Primates in the Classroom

J. Gary Bernhard

PRIMATES IN THE CLASSROOM

An Evolutionary Perspective

on Children's Education

The University of Massachusetts Press

Amherst 1988

Copyright © 1988 by
The University of Massachusetts Press
All rights reserved
Printed in the United States of America
Set in Linotron Times Roman at Meriden-Stinehour Press
Printed by Cushing-Malloy and
bound by John H. Dekker & Sons

Library of Congress Cataloging-in-Publication Data

Bernhard, J. Gary, 1946–
    Primates in the classroom.

    Bibliography: p.
    Includes index.
    1. Education—Social aspects—United States.
2. Learning   3. Socialization.   I. Title.
LC191.4.B47   1988   370.19   87–19153
ISBN 0–87023–610–5 (alk. paper)
ISBN 0–87023–611–3 (pbk.: alk. paper)

British Library Cataloguing in Publication data are available

This book is for JoAnn,

with whom I divide the labor;

for Caitlin and Amanda,

the lodestones of our band;

and for Kalman,

who has been my guide.

Contents

Primates in the Classroom

Introduction

> Let it be born in mind how infinitely complex and
> close-fitting are the mutual relations of all organic
> beings to each other and to their physical conditions
> of life.
> —Charles Darwin, *Origin of Species*

CHILDREN'S EDUCATION AND HUMAN EVOLUTION

In the United States, as in all modern industrial societies, the schools are called upon to perform many of the functions that used to be performed by families and the society at large. Formal education is already a crucial component of a child's socialization in our culture, and there is a trend to begin schooling children at an increasingly early age. It is common knowledge in our society that, if schools are to meet this challenge, they will have to be reformed, but there is no agreement about the direction these reforms should take. I argue in this book that schools must develop specific methods for dealing with certain biologically based social and emotional needs of children. Ideally, formal education in the United States should be reformed along the following lines:

The schools should stop forcing all children to master the same set of abstract reasoning skills in the same ways and in the same time frame.

Children should be allowed to proceed at their own pace, even if this means that they will be learning with children of different ages.

The schools must begin the educational process for all children with activities that focus on natural social relationships and manual skills that all can master, that require cooperative activity, and that are learned primarily through observation, imitation, and spontaneous investigation.

From this educational base, children must be taught cognitive "survival skills" (reading, writing, math), then allowed to select for themselves skill and knowledge areas that are best matched with their inclinations and abilities, whether mechanical, artistic, or cognitive-abstract. The schools must fully support these choices, be able to make the case for a wide range of skills, and come to value these skills equally.

Children must have exposure to a wide range of adult role models in the community, to other children of different ages, and to the elderly.

Teachers should not be trained to operate on the child's level but should be practitioners who, through their own skill and knowledge, provide models for children.

In 1977, when I was the director of Work Experience Classroom, an alternative school in Fitchburg, Massachusetts, I attended a series of open hearings of the North Middlesex Regional School Committee in Townsend, Massachusetts, concerning a "humanistic education" program that had been introduced in the elementary schools of the district. In the course of three meetings I learned that this program consisted of what were called "values clarification exercises," in which children were urged to explore their deepest thoughts and feelings.

On the first night a man stood, identified himself as the father of two children in elementary school, and began to read pronouncements on education from the conservative Heritage Society. Then, his face red with anguish, he clenched his fists and cried, "Give us back our children!" For this man, humanistic education and the system that supported it were undermining the authority of the home and the rights of parents to rear their own children.

It seemed that the man spoke for many in the audience who did not necessarily share his extreme political views but agreed that the primary function of the school is to provide children with basic skills and basic information (and official certifications of achievement), not to probe children's feelings or attempt to influence their moral or political attitudes.

The other side at these hearings was represented by parents and teachers who insisted that the schools were already committed to doing much more than providing basic-skills instruction. During the second meeting, a week later, a teacher from one of the elementary schools in the district took the microphone and said that, because children spend so much of their day in school, it is foolish to think that all they do there is learn how to read, write, and do math. She maintained that attitudes, beliefs, and prejudices were being formed and transmitted in school—whether parents liked it or not—and that by and large the schools were doing a poor job of helping children sort through confusing and sometimes contradictory pressures.

Compromise for these two sides was impossible because their disagreements over the purposes of formal education were differences in kind, not degree. While both groups accused the schools of failing with children, their frameworks for the interpretation of success and failure were so divergent that one group's description of what children need served only to make the other group angry.

This kind of split with regard to education is certainly not new, nor is the fundamental agreement about the poor performance of the public schools. Some fifty years ago John Dewey wrote, "Conservatives as well as radicals in education are profoundly discontented with the present educational situation taken as a whole. There is at least this much agreement among intelligent persons of both schools of educational thought" ([1938] 1963, 89).

The number of combatants has proliferated over the past fifty years. Now, in addition to conservatives and radicals, those who seek consensus in education are pitted against those who believe that conflict is inevitable, given the present social system (Hurn 1985). The liberals who have always believed that formal education makes a social difference must contend with Revisionist claims that the schools have always been in the service of the dominant culture. The polarity has remained. To judge by the North Middlesex School Committee hearings I attended, the extremity of the situation has changed little since Dewey's day. The only agreement remains the perception that education is not working, and the disagreements are so profound and emotional that there is no movement toward a broader understanding of the crucial questions surrounding education and children's learning: What, indeed, is taught in school? What should be taught? In what way should it be taught? What relationships do (or should) the schools bear to other social institutions and to communities? What, after all, is the purpose of schooling in a modern, industrialized nation like the United States?

Every year new studies emerge indicting the schools, the teachers, the entire structure of formal education, and the culture that is represented by such a structure. But the premises upon which these studies are based usually exclude one another (see Hurn 1985 for a concise overview of these polarized positions). Frameworks for educational thought rise like parallel columns in a faulty termite mound, never coming together to form an arch. The red-faced father, fearful that the school was breaking up his home, and the harried teacher, impatient with parents' meddling, will always be at odds (and both will remain at odds with the Marxist academic who studies education) unless we find a new way of viewing children's learning and formal education—a perspective that enables us either to join some of these ideological columns at the top or to create a wholly new foundation upon which we can begin to build different kinds of schools.

By the time I attended the North Middlesex hearings I had been a teacher-administrator in Work Experience Classroom for two years, and I had witnessed some remarkable things. I had seen a high school dropout with a second-grade reading level reach a ninth-grade reading level after one year in the school. I had seen teenagers from wretched home environments learn to function more effectively as members of a class, a carpentry crew, or a circle of friends. I had seen curiosity rekindle in the most cynical young men and women and satisfaction for good work grow in grossly underpaid staff. Even as the North Middlesex hearings recounted everyone's dissatisfaction with formal education, I thought of how education (as I knew it in the alternative school) had made profound and positive differences in the lives of many people I worked with, and in mine as well.

This study began as an attempt to account for the successes I saw in Work Experience Classroom. It explores the gap between emotional and cognitive dimensions of learning, between the experiential and the intellectual, and between the social and the individual aspects of how and why children learn. A couple of years after the North Middlesex hearings, I became interested in human evolution. A friend introduced me to the implications of viewing human beings as creatures who evolved in the same way other creatures on earth evolved, and ultimately my investigations led me back to education and to my experiences in the alternative school. By then I had left Work Experience Classroom, but as I learned about other primate societies, early humans, and contemporary hunting-and-gathering peoples, I became convinced that the secret of the alternative school's success was that we had unknowingly stumbled into fundamental human learning adaptations. We had made it possible for young people to learn what they needed to learn in social environments, by means of the activities that have formed the core of primate and human learning for millions of years.

It is clear to me now that the fundamental purposes of human learning in a modern technological society are exactly the same as they have been in primate and human societies for millions of years. The young need to learn how to become adult members of a social group. In a culture in which there are so many conflicting messages about what adulthood and competence are, this task is very difficult. But for most of our existence as a species, adulthood has meant knowing how to survive in the physical environment and thrive in the social environment. And thriving in the social environment meant "figuring out," discovering, certain fundamental relationships: male to male, female to female, male to female, parent to child, and young to old.

Underlying all these social relationships are ancient emotional systems that are connected not only with the relationships themselves but also with the process of figuring them out. We human beings, like other social primates, are motivated to belong to a group. At the same time we are motivated to acquire and advance an individual identity, to be recognized and have status in the group. We are also motivated to explore our physical and social environment. As early human children figured out their social world, they learned about cooperation and reciprocity. At the same time they learned about assertiveness, personal identity, and status. The activities that facilitated this learning were pleasurable and exciting, so our ancestors were urged to engage in them often.

Becoming an adult, for most of human existence, has meant coming to an understanding of how the need to belong to a group and the need to have personal identity fit together. In the social environments in which our species evolved, these needs coexisted in a dynamic balance, so the young found their fit with others and themselves as a normal consequence of living. This discovery process also promoted an understanding of how to subsist in the physical environment, how to choose and live with mates and friends, how to live with relatives, how to raise children, how to dispute with others, how to resolve disputes, and so forth.

The old social balances that have characterized hominid and human societies for so long have been disrupted more and more severely as humans have discovered ways to separate the collective and the individual. The emotional needs, however, remain. They are part of our biology as a species: we need to belong to a group, we need to have a personal identity in that group, and we need to explore our relationship with the environment.

The young people who attended Work Experience Classroom were confused about many of the fundamental human relationships. They did not know whom to trust or even what obligations and rewards trust implied. Cooperation was valuable only when an individual could achieve something immediate by working with others. Though the desire to establish reciprocal relations was obvious and powerful, many of these youngsters had never experienced genuine reciprocity. They were, therefore, terrified of "owing" someone and gave to others only when they were assured of a quick payback.

With the balancing forces of trust and reciprocity largely missing from their lives, these adolescents spent much of their time aggressively trying to establish an individual identity and acquire status in the groups they were part of. But the models of adulthood they had encountered had been, for the most part, treacherous (in the case of their parents and relatives) or unrealistic (in the case of schoolteachers, social workers, and movie characters). These teenagers thus had to construct an identity whole out of what they saw around them—on television, for instance— and what seemed to be valued by their peers. They were dumbfounded by their sexuality, for there was no meaningful adult context in which to place maleness or femaleness or sex. Both boys and girls were presented with overblown, sometimes distasteful, sometimes demeaning, examples of what being men and women was like. Both sexes balked at "growing up" if they had to become what was offered by their society.

Even though some of these young people had (or were going to have) children of their own while they were in Work Experience Classroom, it was clear that little in their lives had prepared them for being parents or caring for their own children. Most of them had come from families in which there was no balance between belonging and individuality. Then, too, they had been isolated in age-mate groups in school for many years and knew almost nothing about babies and young children—even if they had younger siblings at home. This same school isolation also made it more difficult for them to find out about another important aspect of adulthood: growing old. They thought they would remain the way they were forever.

These difficulties of adolescent life were perceived long ago. In 1961, James Coleman's *Adolescent Society* demonstrated beyond doubt that our efforts at socializing adolescents in the schools were falling seriously short of young people's needs. As Coleman says,

> The results of this research are disturbing to one concerned with the ability of an open society to raise its children today and in the future. This was once a task largely carried out within the family or in local places of work, a task with which the larger society had little need to concern itself. But the rationalization of society more and more inhibits the "natural" processes, by separating the adolescent off into institutions of his own, and insulating him from adults' work and adults' perspective. The adolescent remains in these institutions, treated as a child, for a longer and longer period, while he gains social sophistication earlier and earlier. (P. 311)

Surely Erik Erikson verbalized the experiences of thousands of teachers and parents when, in *Identity: Youth and Crisis* (1968), he wrote

> Should a young person feel that the environment tries to deprive him too radically of all the forms of expression which permit him to develop and integrate the next step [towards personal identity], he may resist with the wild strength encountered in animals who are suddenly forced to defend their lives. For, indeed, in the social jungle of human existence there is no feeling of being alive without a sense of identity (P. 130)

I find these classic studies of youth in modern society interesting because both reveal the presence of an assumption about human nature but do not deal directly with the issue of what is natural. Coleman, Erikson, and many others who have looked at children's learning, education, and socialization have accurately identified the problems but have always approached the reasons for the existence of these problems from a historical rather than from an evolutionary point of view. Coleman, for example, refers to "natural" processes, but for some reason he puts quotation marks around the word *natural*. Erikson likewise compares the response of thwarted adolescents to wild animals and mentions the "jungle of human existence." But his recommendations for reform and change are consistently historical and psychoanalytical rather than evolutionary.

These hidden assumptions about human nature in general and about children's education in particular have plagued the social sciences from the beginning and are in part responsible for the fragmented and polarized state of educational thought. As I hope to make clear in this book, unless we have a sense of the emotional and behavioral characteristics that we humans actually do share as a species, our recommendations for improvement, growth, change, equality, and so forth will always emphasize a particular ideology or a particular personal experience rather than basic human needs and the experience of the species.

An evolutionary perspective can give us a first glimpse at *why* the problems identified by so many are indeed problems. In some ways, then, there is really nothing very new about what is said in this book. It is still true, twenty-five years later, that, when adolescents are insulated from adults' work and adults' perspectives, serious problems result. But now we may begin to see why this social arrangement causes the young so much distress and has such a negative effect on their learning. And we may also begin to see why so many attempted educational reforms have been so futile.

Human beings best learn what they need to know in groups that allow them to feel simultaneously secure in their belonging to the group and confident that they are regarded as individuals by other group members. My experience as a teacher of reading, writing, and math has shown me that such a social environment for learning is as important for the acquisition of intellectual skill as it is for the acquisition of social skill. Other "survival" competencies in the modern world—such as manual and machine abilities, knowledge of materials, and artistic skills—are, in the initial stages, also learned best in this environment.

In all cultures children need to discover what social relations are in an environment with adults who *know* how these relations work. But in our day children are *not* allowed to make discoveries in an environment with adults, many of whom are themselves confused about how to behave. Even so, we still approach each social situation with the expectation that the dynamic balance between belonging and personal status will hold, because our species evolved over the course of millions of years in societies that were characterized by both collective security and individual opportunity.

In these primate, hominid, and human societies, the young learned by doing—by observing, imitating, playing, and investigating—and these learning activities were perfectly matched with the "subject matter." Our ancestors, as children, were powerfully motivated to encounter their world. They derived pleasure and excitement from novelty and the satisfaction of curiosity. As they watched and played and tried things out, they gained survival skill, confidence, and knowledge; they learned how to effect delicate social balances and were cast in roles they would grow into as adults.

Without knowing it, the teachers, counselors, and job supervisors of Work Experience Classroom created an environment in which the young could both belong in the school and retain (or re-create) an individual identity. We encouraged exploration, and at the same time we demanded, as adults, that our students pay attention to social rules and values. We tried to foster respect for a wide variety of individual skills and simultaneously pressed the virtues of cooperation.

Teachers, parents, counselors, and others have frequently stumbled into similar spectacular learning situations with the young. We know something is working, but we are not sure what it is. And we tell ourselves that, if we only knew how to create those moments, we would do it all the time. In this book I have tried to present my understanding of why the magic works: why great teachers are great, why children who understand the reasons for performing a particular activity excel, and why children made cynical by an unnatural environment can recover the pleasure of learning and participating. I have also tried to present my understanding of why there is so little magic in our institutions of formal education: why children who "learn" information all day in environments that tell them nothing about adult social life often give up exploring, and at the same time, why schools that refuse to "impose" adult models of reality may confuse rather than liberate children.

THE STUDY OF HUMAN EVOLUTION

The search for a firmer foundation for educational thought begins with an investigation into human evolution. But this field itself is fraught with as many psychological and political problems as any educational study.

All evolutionary processes take place in the context of what Waddington (1957) called the "epigenetic system." This system is made up of the *genotype* (the genetic structure of the individual and of the gene pool within the basic reproducing group, or deme), the *phenotype* (the observable characteristics of the individual), and the *environment* in which the organism lives. The genotype includes a wide range of potentialities that are not necessarily realized in the phenotype, the phenotype includes not only physical attributes but also developmental and behavioral characteristics, and the environment for animals that live in groups is social as well as physical.

Evolution is, in its most basic terms, the interaction of these three elements in what is known as a *stochastic* process. A system or sequence of events is said to be stochastic when it consists of both random events and regulatory mechanisms that select certain events rather than others. Mutations are apparently random events, and the characteristics of the environment act as regulatory mechanisms that eliminate negative or unfavorable alternatives that are realized in the phenotype.

If a mutation in the genotype is realized in the phenotype, the organism must survive in the environment with its new characteristic. Darwinian *fitness* means that, if a variation in the genome is negative, the organism will either die or not reproduce or will produce fewer offspring than individuals without the new characteristic. But if the variation is positive the organism will be more fit, that is, will reproduce more successfully, and will thus perpetuate the mutation in the gene pool of the species.

In this general description of evolution, *adaptation* may be viewed as the spread and stabilization of characteristics through a population in a particular environment. A successful adaptation leads to a kind of homeostasis within the deme in a given environment, which will hold until either the environment changes or some more successful variation in the genotype occurs and is reflected in the phenotype.

Few would argue with these fundamental principles of evolution. But when we attempt to apply these principles to human behavior, r ?ed, and capacity, we enter a new realm, a kind of "thought warp." The processes that have produced the fruit fly *Drosophila* are the same processes that have produced human beings on earth. Because we may now radically change the physical environment it is critical to our survival as a species (and the survival of many other species) that we comprehend our evolutionary origin. However we continue to behave as though we had never heard of Charles Darwin.

We may adopt such a stance, in part, because an evolutionary perspective is a perspective on *everything* related to human beings. It is a way of seeing not only children's learning but all human interaction, history, psychology, the relationship of humans to the natural environment, the effects of technology, and so forth. Assumptions about human nature abound in every aspect of human social life and thought, as in Coleman's study of adolescence, and attempts to define the "nature of children's learning" may strike many of these chords simultaneously. Indeed, any perception about the way children learn as members of the human species threatens at every moment to expand into a perception about Western society or child-rearing practices in modern industrial societies or male-female relations. Gigantic, unwieldy hypotheses thrust themselves forward for consideration, and once entertained they tend to force even larger, more generalized, hypotheses. Such perceptions, of course, also threaten established paradigms of learning and education.

For me, the acquisition of an evolutionary perspective on children's learning has been a paradigm shift as described by Thomas Kuhn in *The Structure of Scientific Revolutions* (1970). The framework this perspective affords is substantially different from previous investigative frameworks in education, and this same paradigm can be applied to every other aspect of human life. As Kuhn says, a paradigm shift takes a considerable amount of time and meets with a great deal of resistance. Surely one can stumble into a pitfall or crash into a controversy at every step.

For this reason it is a good idea to identify some of the major areas of uncertainty and disagreement that come up in a discussion of evolution and human learning. I cannot address all the subtleties of evolutionary disagreement here, but I hope that by presenting some of the best-known problems in the study of human evolution I can avoid misunderstandings later.

HUMAN BEHAVIOR AND EVOLUTION

The term *evolutionary perspective* calls forth a variety of responses in people. Some are offended by the term; others are intrigued. Some feel that their religious beliefs are compromised by an evolutionary frame of reference, while others see our primate past as a justification for the existence of hierarchy, aggression, and violence in the contemporary world.

We owe much of the confusion about evolution and its connection with modern human behavior to Herbert Spencer, who applied Darwin's description of organic evolution to human behavior and social development. In his *Principles of Psychology* (1870–1872), Spencer invented the phrase "survival of the fittest" and maintained that the selection processes postulated by Darwin for animal species were also at work in human societies. Human beings, as products of the processes of evolution, were constrained by their biological structures and, like other animals, had to be part of the "struggle for existence." Spencer saw the struggles between different human societies as a reflection of this biological heritage and assumed that human history demonstrated that some societies are more fit than others. This fitness, according to Spencer, could be observed in the relative power a given society has in the world community. Weak societies are less fit than strong societies.

Spencer was wrong for a number of reasons that have been pointed out numerous times (e.g., Dobzhansky 1955; Gould 1979). Although there are certainly relationships between biological evolution and cultural development, an understanding of these relationships requires more than a simple superimposition of the concepts and language of organic evolution onto human behavior and social interaction.

First, there is no necessary correlation between social success and reproductive success.* Being a powerful cultural figure does not guarantee a large number of offspring. Indeed, having children can actually hinder one's social success in a modern technological society.

Second, the time frame of cultural development and change is so short that it can in no way be likened to the time frame of biological evolution. When we speak of "evolutionary processes" we are speaking of processes that take place over hundreds of thousands or millions of years. The incorporation of physiological and behavioral characteristics into the genetic structure of a species should not be confused with timely responses of individuals and groups to changing environments — whether these responses are cultural themes, customs, or modes of interpretation.

Finally, in the assumption that the survival of some must come at the expense of others, social Darwinism ignores elements of balance and equilibrium that are also associated with biological evolution in general and, as I try to demonstrate in this book, with human evolution in particular.

In spite of the fact that social Darwinism is a plainly false correlation, it continues to exert a certain attraction. One often reads, for example, that those who do not adapt to the Information Age will be left behind. The implication here is that some people are capable of making so-called adaptations to new environmental stresses induced by the Information Age and that some are not. Those who cannot adapt are supposedly less fit than those who can. This belief is sheer nonsense in a biological sense and completely ignores questions of opportunity and value. Nevertheless, the conviction is surprisingly common even among people who may know something about biological evolution.

So manifestly dangerous is a simpleminded correlation of biological structure with social superiority that the term *evolutionary perspective* can set off a series of negative responses in those who have seen the abuses and can predict potential abuses of Spencer's idea. The thought that contemporary human behavior and capacity may be determined by genetic structure or that destructive behavior is natural in the context of the human evolutionary past is unacceptable to people who see the need for profound change in human social interaction and organization. For

---

*Of course at the most extreme end of the relationship there is a correlation: the victims of a genocidal purge by a dominant culture will surely reproduce less effectively than the members of the dominant culture.

these critics of social Darwinism it is often easier to avoid the human evolutionary heritage altogether. The notion that there are "biological constraints" on human beings, rooted in an evolutionary past, conjures up Hitler, eugenics, and slavery.

The problem with this critique is that, while it justly condemns social Darwinism, it is also likely to produce intellectual models for social change that ignore crucial needs that are the product of human evolution. The sad irony here is that some of our most serious problems are the result of our losing touch with our evolutionary heritage through the development of increasingly sophisticated intellectual and technological systems. To demand a reform of a particular system without acknowledging the origin and antiquity of the needs such reforms are supposed to address is like heading into the wilderness with neither woodcraft nor compass. It is likely that we will get lost.

The so-called sociobiology debate (e.g., Caplan 1978), which pits those who insist on a formidable genetic component of modern human behavior against those who worry about how a genetic theory of behavior might be misused, is a kind of red herring in this question, for it urges the old nature/nurture dichotomy. When one uses the term *selfish genes* (Dawkins 1976), it is impossible to avoid an aura of genetic determinism that no disclaimers can dispel—and an extremely complex process is oversimplified. On the other hand, if human beings have emerged from the same processes that shaped the duck's webbed foot, there is no doubt that our behavior in any environment is influenced by components that are biologically based. It is as foolish to claim that the evolutionary heritage of humanity exerts no significant pressure upon modern human behavior as it is to claim that modern human behavior is determined by genetic structures.

I consider learning to be a complex of activities that reflect both genetically based motivations common to the entire species and the demands of the environment in which individuals exist. Human beings are cultural beings. This means that the environment in which the young grow and develop is profoundly affected by the language, social organization, ideas, customs, and history of those with whom the young live and come in contact. But the impact of the cultural environment on the learning of the young does not cancel out biologically based characteristics of learning; it only greatly complicates the context in which these human learning characteristics are located.

We surely do have a lot of trouble seeing ourselves as the products of evolution. Nevertheless, gaining a vision of ourselves that begins before recent history may be the best chance we have of not repeating the worst mistakes of that history. If we humans evolved we must share more than an opposable thumb with other primates; if we have been foragers for 99 percent of our existence, we may be able to learn a great deal about who we are and why we feel and behave the way we do from contemporary foragers. Most important for the purposes of this book, if we have become a species as other forms of life on earth have, we learn best in ways that are characteristic of our species, not in ways that are imposed by transient educational fashions.

This study is presented in three parts. Part 1 investigates the social and emotional contexts of learning and the activities of learning in higher primate groups. Part 2 is concerned with these learning contexts and activities as they have probably existed for most of the history of the human species. Part 3 explores the ways in which these learning contexts and activities have changed in rather recent human history, describes the problems that these changes have created in children's education, and offers suggestions for educational reform from an evolutionary perspective.

Part I

The Primate Heritage

I

The Social Context of Primate Learning

THE primate order is divided into two suborders, Prosimii (lemurs, lorises, and tarsirs) and Anthropoidea (monkeys, apes, and humans). Anthropoidea is further divided into the platyrrhines (New World monkeys) and the catarrhines (higher primates, including baboons, macaques, gorillas, chimpanzees, and humans). The evidence from molecular biology indicates that humans, chimpanzees, and gorillas are relatively close cousins (Sarich 1968). Our evolutionary line may have diverged from these fellow catarrhines no more than five to seven million years ago.

PRIMATE STUDIES AND HUMAN EVOLUTION

We humans have always been curious about our relationship to the higher primates. The Semang of Malaysia call the large apes of the rain forest *orang hutan*, "man of the forest." The Mbuti of the Ituri forest have a legend that the chimpanzees had fire before humans and that Mbuti women stole it from them. In the West the obvious resemblances between higher primates and humans have encouraged a great deal of study and speculation. However, there are some potential pitfalls in the study of our primate cousins, which I would like to address before beginning a description of primate social life and its relationship to the learning of the young.

One difficulty encountered when looking for relationships between humans and other primates is the question of which correspondences apply to the relationship and which do not. There are a number of general and specific characteristics of catarrhines (Old World monkeys, apes, and humans) that seem to be connected in one way or another with human characteristics, and it is tempting to pick and choose among them in the creation of hypotheses. These similarities look like familiar landmarks in the often bewildering complexity of evolutionary relatedness, but it is difficult to tell whether such correspondences are actually *homologous* (that is, due to evolutionary relatedness) or *analogous* (that is, fortuitous and arising independently, perhaps in response to similar environmental pressures).

Gibbons, for example, form monogamous family groups of a male, a female, and their young offspring (Ellefson 1968), and one is drawn to compare the social life of gibbons with the family structures of human beings. No doubt the comparison is all the more compelling because monogamous male-female dyads are prevalent in many human societies and are usually idealized. Nevertheless, though the gibbon pair-bonding bears this superficial similarity to human pair-bonding, it is only analogous, according to most primatologists: "The gibbon 'family' is a common pattern for small birds and mammals in the tropics and does not represent a predecessor to the human family" (Lancaster 1975, 34).

The hamadryas baboon's social organization is based on what has been called the harem; that is, a group of females guarded by a single dominant male (Kummer 1971). The baboon is of great interest to those engaged in the study of human evolution because most species are ground dwelling, as were the ancient hominids. Indeed, some researchers have found in baboon social arrangements models for human social life (e.g., Kummer 1971, 152). But as with gibbon social arrangements and human family life, any correspondences between the hamadryas harem structure and human dominance hierarchies (or human harems, for that matter) must be examined with great care. Many believe that the hamadryas harem is "not so much a unit adapted for mating as it is for foraging in an environment of scarce and scattered food resources" (Lancaster 1975, 33). In the end it seems that a good approach to the study of other primates for the light that can be shed on human learning is not to match characteristics (either physiological or behavioral) one-for-one but to describe the *kinds* of relationships, behavior and activities that occur relevant to learning in other catarrhine societies.

Although there is considerable variation among primate species in terms of the size of subsistence and breeding groups, the range such groups cover in their search for food, and the permeability between groups of the same species, it is possible to view societies of Old World monkeys and apes in terms of "axes of social organization" that provide a general and flexible framework within which major themes of primate sociality — and thus primate learning — may be identified. Lancaster describes five such axes: (1) dominance and dominance hierarchies, (2) the mother-infant bond and the matrifocal subunit, (3) the sexual bond between males and females, (4) the separation of roles by sex, and (5) the separation of roles by age.

> They are like themes which are woven together to form a pattern unique for each species. Sometimes certain of these axes will be emphasized in meeting the challenge of a particular environmental problem confronting the species or perhaps only the social group. Sometimes, too, a particular social group may have a social tradition in which one of these themes may dominate whereas its neighbors will have another. (1975, 13)

Obviously, these kinds of relationships also characterize human sociality, and with some modification (i.e., I combine 3 and 4 above) I use this approach in this chapter.

For young social primates of all species, including humans, learning means a great deal more than becoming familiar with the external environment and accumulating information that contributes to individual survival. Primate societies are complex organizations in which individual animals must know a great deal in order to be socially competent. And social competence is often the key to survival for individuals and the group.

The relations between males and males, between females and females, between mothers and their offspring, between males and females, and between the young and mature animals of a group constitute a network of interaction that forms the social environment in which a young primate learns and is much of the *content* of that learning as well. The major purposes of primate learning are today (and were, no doubt, before the evolution of the human species) to prepare the young for survival in the physical environment and to enable them to discover the social relationships and roles they will encounter as adults. In addition, the activities through which young monkeys and apes acquire skill and information, gain an individual identity, and discover their relationship to the group are perfectly appropriate to these learning tasks.

This chapter reviews the social relationships that provide so much of the form and content of the learning that a young primate must do. Much of the material in this chapter may at first seem irrelevant to a study of children's education in a modern industrial society, but I ask the reader's indulgence as I lay the foundation for connections that will become clear later on.

DOMINANCE AND HIERARCHY: MALE TO MALE, FEMALE TO FEMALE

One of the most important sets of behavior a young monkey or ape needs to learn is associated with dominance and hierarchy. These activities are crucial, for they are related to the availability of resources, sexuality, and the protection of individual offspring and of the group as a whole. They are thus vital to the creation of a secure environment within which the young can have the time and confidence to learn all that must be learned. In addition dominance and hierarchy are primary components of what Chance and Jolly (1970) call the "attention structure" of the group—that is, the way in which an animal's attention is deployed.

In recent years our understanding of dominance and the role it plays in primate social life and the learning of the young has grown more complex with better information about how groups of monkeys and apes live in the wild. For example, it has become clear that dominance in some societies is not as individualistic as it was once thought to be. DeVore (1965) observed the formation of a coalition among baboons in which six individuals joined together to increase their collective status. Researchers have also determined that, although dominance relations are usually seen at their most flamboyant and potentially dangerous in males, females have their own dominance hierarchies and rituals for determining and enforcing rank (Hall and DeVore 1965). In addition, it seems that the character of male and female dominance hierarchies is different and that these structures serve different purposes in the group. In some primate societies (e.g., macaques and vervet monkeys), the single most important component of an individual's rank is its *mother's* rank (Kawamura 1958; Lancaster 1971), probably because the female hierarchy is more stable and enduring than the male hierarchy (see below). At the same time, a male's status often rises or falls according to his individual behavior.

In order for dominance hierarchies to be useful rather than destructive, they must allow the animals in a group to predict the outcome of a wide range of encounters (Kummer 1971) so that time and energy are not wasted in fighting that could lead to injury or death (which in turn could, in some species, leave the entire group unprotected). For this reason most aggression between males and males and between females and females is ritualized (Eibl-Eibesfeldt 1971). The emphasis is placed on display and threat, with the result that all-out battles are rare.

Because the dominance hierarchies of higher primates are so complex, the young must learn more than the rituals themselves; they must also explore the limits to which the rituals can be pushed. The intensity and danger of these encounters vary from situation to situation and from species to species. Newly dominant gorilla males have been observed killing the offspring of the previously dominant silverback male.

Although much of the dominance hierarchy in higher primate societies is determined through matrifocal relations and ritualized aggression, individual animals may discover new behavior that has a significant effect on the entire group structure. Jane van Lawick-Goodall (1971) describes the remarkable use of empty kerosene cans by Mike, a young male chimpanzee, to enhance his aggressive display and thus his status in the group. This animal was at the bottom of the dominance hierarchy, according to van Lawick-Goodall, when one day he decided to try something new.

A group of five adult males, including top-ranking Goliath, David Graybeard, and the huge Rodolf, were grooming each other. The session had been going on for some twenty minutes. Mike was sitting about thirty yards apart from them, frequently staring toward the group, occasionally idly grooming himself.

All at once Mike calmly walked over to our tent and took hold of an empty kerosene can by the handle. Then he picked up a second can and, walking upright, returned to the place where he had been sitting. Armed with his two cans Mike continued to stare toward the other males. After a few minutes he began to rock from side to side. At first the movement was almost imperceptible. . . . Gradually he rocked more vigorously, his hair slowly began to stand erect, and then, softly at first, he started a series of pant-hoots. As he called, Mike got to his feet and suddenly he was off, charging toward the group of males, hitting the two cans ahead of him. The cans, together with Mike's crescendo of hooting, made the most appalling racket: no wonder the erstwhile peaceful males rushed out of the way. (Pp. 121–23).

Using this technique, Mike rose through the dominance hierarchy of the group to the foremost position in a short period of time. Van Lawick-Goodall speculates that Mike's use of the cans was "an indication of superior intelligence," and it is fascinating to contemplate the role that intelligence and learning may play in dominance hierarchies among higher primates. Apparently, a good deal more than simple brute force is involved.

Other behavior related to dominance that requires some learning of the young has to do with the protection of individual offspring (in the case of females) and of the group in general (in the case of males). The ferocity of maternal protective behavior in primate societies is well known and might be considered wholly instinctual. But Lancaster observed a group of female vervet monkeys form a coalition to protect an infant from a fractious male. Arboreal species that must fear predation (not including the chimpanzee, who seems to have only humans to fear) often use a complex protective strategy that Kummer (1971) calls the "patas pattern." A male diverts the attention of a potential predator from the group by making loud aggressive displays while the other animals slip silently away.

The dominance hierarchy and the rules of dominance that have evolved over millions of years in primate societies stand both as part of the social *content* for primate young to discover and master and as important *deter-*

minants of the learning environment. But there are other significant relationships in higher primate societies.

THE MATRIFOCAL UNIT

Until the mid-1960s most field studies were short enterprises that tended
to miss some of the more subtle elements of primate social organization.
Long-term studies (e.g., van Lawick-Goodall 1965, 1971; Koyama
1970), however, have shown that perhaps the most pervasive and enduring
elements of primate social organization are those that revolve around the
relationship between mothers and their offspring.

More than twenty years ago the Harlows demonstrated the importance
and strength of the bonds between rhesus macaque mothers and infants
in laboratory studies. Infant macaques were raised in varying degrees of
isolation: with biological mothers, with surrogate mothers made of cloth,
with surrogates of wire, and in bare wire cages without any surrogate
mother. In addition to varying the amount of contact between infants and
their mothers or various mother surrogates, the Harlows varied the
amount of exposure these infants had to peers. The results of these
experiments and others in succeeding years are summarized by Lewis
and Sackett (1980).

> Broadly speaking, the degree to which rearing departs from situa-
> tions in which mothers and peers are freely available to the develop-
> ing rhesus monkey predicts the degree to which that monkey will
> be abnormal or deviant in most behaviors as a juvenile and adult.
> Isolate and wire cage reared animals are abnormal in all areas of
> behavior, except for the ability to perform on standard monkey
> learning tests. In fact, learning performance does not appear to
> differ between rearing conditions ranging from wild-born to total
> isolate. Thus, early rearing experiences involving social privation
> appear not to influence basic "intellectual abilities." However, the
> deprivation-raised animal's *willingness to perform on learning
> tasks is markedly deviant* [my italics].
>   Deprivation of maternal contact [but with adequate exposure to

peers] during infancy yields rhesus monkeys that show heightened self-orality and fear behaviors, although play and aggression are fairly normal, as are sexual and maternal behaviors. . . .

Rearing monkeys with mothers but with no peer contact produces animals that shy away from physical contact with other monkeys, showing hyperaggression toward others when touched but apparently normal sexual and maternal behavior. (Pp. 116–17)

Field studies have corroborated the laboratory findings concerning the importance of mother-infant contact in the development of young primates. In many societies the offspring continue to recognize their mothers into adulthood. Sexual relationships between mothers and sons are exceedingly rare among higher primate groups for which such information has been gathered, though father-daughter and brother-sister relations are quite common (Itani 1972). Sade (1965) has shown that, although the very close and intense relationship between mother and infant changes after weaning, it does not end there.

The importance of the complex of relationships that revolve around the mother in many primate societies has been demonstrated by studies of group movements and "traveling arrangements." Kummer (1971) reports that, although mountain gorilla groups appear to be led by a single silverback male, most other primate groups are "led jointly by several adults," both male and female (p. 63). Lancaster (1975) suggests that the greater stability of females as members of most primate groups probably provides them with a more accurate knowledge of the group's range than the males (who are usually more mobile between groups) are likely to have. Rowell's observations have led him to believe that decisions about when and where a baboon troop goes are most probably made by the older, higher-ranking females in the group's center. These messages are then relayed throughout the group by males, usually those closely related to these "indicator females"—brothers or sons (1969).

As noted above, long-term studies of primate societies such as those of the Japanese Monkey Center (e.g., Koyama 1970) indicate that the status of individual animals in a group is intimately connected with the position of large-scale "matrilinear geneologies" that remain relatively stable for long periods of time, and Lancaster (1971) has observed similar relationships among vervet monkeys. In most primate societies the offspring of high-ranking females tend to be more dominant (whether male or female), while the offspring of females with lower rank tend to remain at that level (Harlow and Harlow 1965). We are only beginning to understand the relationships between dominance hierarchies and the complex of attachments surrounding matrifocal units, but it is clear that "matrifocality is a principle of primate social grouping which is different from but just as important as a dominance hierarchy, and in many primate societies these principles form crosscutting ties which bind individuals into the social group" (Lancaster 1975, 31).

So in addition to learning the rules (and the limits) of dominance hierarchies, young primates learn "who they are" in relationship to their mothers and the status their mothers have in the society at large. The matrifocal unit provides the young with a secure environment from which to venture forth into the outside world. A great deal of the information and skill a young primate must learn in order to survive in the physical and social environment is transmitted through the "matrifocal pathways" (see chapter 3).

MALE-FEMALE RELATIONS AND ROLES

In most primate species the bonds between adult males and females are strong only during female estrus. At that time male and female behavior alters dramatically in every species, and among the chimpanzee, preferences that seem to be reciprocal may develop between males and females. Van Lawick-Goodall (1971) describes two such arrangements. These pairings apparently last for the length of the estrus cycle only, however, after which the animals go their separate ways.

The two major exceptions to this generalization are the gibbon and the hamadryas baboon, mentioned above, and it is interesting to note that, even though these primates live in groups in which the same males and females are bound together for long periods of time, nothing resembling reciprocal bonds has developed. The hamadryas baboon male jealously guards his harem from intruders, but the hamadryas females have no loyalty to the male and are quite willing to mate with any available male when in estrus (Kummer 1971).

The specific roles that males and females play in primate societies vary according to species and, of course, to the environment in which the animals live. The male hamadryas baboon bullies females into following along and keeps checking periodically to see that they are close behind, while both male and female chimpanzees pretty much go their own way and move among semipermeable groups. Macaque females may band together against a male if he has frightened an infant, but hamadryas baboon females demonstrate no such behavior. Nevertheless, it is possible to identify broad male-female roles that occur in all primate societies: females have specialized roles in relation to the care and welfare of the young, and males have specialized roles with respect to group protection from external danger. As noted above, both roles require learning on the part of the young for competence.

The females of any catarrhine society are the primary parents of any infants that are born into the group, and interest in the young seems to be generalized throughout the female population of any primate society. There is considerable evidence that primate mothers must *learn* their role rather than simply respond to instinctual cues concerning the welfare of the young, and the generalized female interest in infants facilitates this learning (see chapter 2).

The primary specialized role of males in catarrhine societies is group protection. Males of all species do spend time with infants, play with them, and are interested in them generally. In addition adult males will occasionally adopt orphaned infants, often their own siblings (see van Lawick-Goodall 1971). However, they apparently form no lasting relationship with the young. Their interest in juveniles, particularly other males, quickly wanes as the latter reach maturity. Mature males should thus probably be "regarded as generalized fathers; they show affectional resonses to members of their social group but do not show them differentially to their own or to other children" (Harlow and Harlow 1965, 330). Male protectiveness, like male affection, is generalized to the entire group.

The care of the young and the protection of the group are the primary role specializations of females and males in primate societies, but there are other roles, related to dominance and the matrifocal unit, that are divided to some degree (but with different emphases in different species) between males and females. In many dominance-oriented species, for example, males play what are called "indicator roles" (Chance and Jolly,

1970). They relay information to every member of the group through the attention structure. At the same time, as we have seen, dominant females may play similar indicator and information-disseminator roles in other primate species. The information is relayed to other members of the group through a different network. In some species the dominant males play an enforcer role in order to maintain social order (Harlow and Harlow 1965), while, as noted above, in other species coalitions of females may at times perform a similar function.

Part of the complexity of the learning that young primates must do concerns the gender roles they acquire as they grow. Although these roles appear to be rather undeveloped among most species (compared with male-female roles in human societies), there are some remarkable examples of male-female role specialization among chimpanzees (and to a lesser extent among baboons) that are of particular interest, since they may be precursors of behavior that for many years was thought to be exclusively human in the primate world: namely, the use and manufacture of tools and the procurement, distribution, and eating of meat.

It has long been known that chimpanzees (and other primates) use tools in various activities. Male chimps and gorillas, and occasionally baboons, pick up sticks to brandish in display and often throw sticks and stones at intruders. Since van Lawick-Goodall first observed chimps using sticks as tools to probe into termite mounds, the behavior has been witnessed in several populations throughout Africa. Not only do the animals use sticks, they *modify* them for the purpose as well. In other words, chimpanzees make tools with what can only be a conception of their future use.

Only in recent years have apparent gender specializations been observed in these activities involving tool use. Boesch and Boesch (1981) observed such a specialization in connection with the cracking of coula and panda nuts by chimpanzees in the Tia National Park of the Ivory Coast. These animals use stone or wood hammers and anvils to crack open the nuts. The panda nuts are so hard that only stone hammers may be used, and the animals carry these hammers rather long distances in order to crack the nuts—again, evidence for some sort of forethought. Sometimes the coula nuts are cracked in the trees, a difficult task that requires considerable agility.

The Boesches discovered that two techniques—the cracking of panda nuts and the cracking of coula nuts in the trees—were used almost exclusively by females. Further evidence for a gender specialization in activities connected with tool use has been provided by McGrew (1979), who noted that female chimpanzees spend more time digging for termites than males do.

Males engage in predatory behavior or hunting more than females do. For the most part higher primates are independent foragers for fruit, nuts, leaves, and other vegetable material. Many species eat insects and eggs, but the group characteristically moves through its range at a leisurely pace, each animal pausing to eat whatever it finds immediately. There is usually nothing set aside for another time or carried from one place to another (although the carrying of food by chimpanzees has been observed [Harding and Teleki 1981]). However, since meat eating and then hunting by chimpanzees were observed by van Lawick-Goodall in the Gombe National Park in the early 1960s, these activities have been witnessed so often that "Gombe chimpanzees emerge as competent, skilled predators whose impact on the local fauna is greater than anyone expected" (Teleki 1981, 327).

Teleki distinguishes between "opportunistic" predatory behavior, in which a prey animal is flushed and caught by the chimp that comes upon it, and deliberate "searching or stalking activities [that] precede the capture" (1974, 50). Van Lawick-Goodall (1971) describes what seemed to be a remarkably well-coordinated hunt in which several males participated. Strum (1981) has observed what she called simple and complex hunting among baboons in Kenya. She reports that adult males, females, and juveniles all captured prey during the period of her observation but that only adult males engaged in complex hunting. Teleki reports that "less than 4% of the chimpanzee kills documented in Gombe National Park have been made by adult females and adolescent males" (1981, 335).

One of the most remarkable aspects of chimpanzee hunting and meat-eating behavior is in the way meat is divided within the troop. Other animals approach the adult male or males that have made the kill and beg a piece of the carcass, using a characteristic open-palm gesture (van Lawick-Goodall 1965, 1971). Other males, females, juveniles, and even infants have been observed begging in this way—often for long periods of time until rewarded—and van Lawick-Goodall has concluded that because "meat is a much liked, much prized food item" (1971, 207), it elicits from the whole troop behavior that is radically different from the usual subsistence behavior: the hunting, the begging gestures, and what may be considered the sharing of food.

We will never know for certain whether this gender-specific behavior surrounding subsistence and tool use represents behavior that existed in prehominid primates four million years ago. We may be certain, however, that the learning that the young of all primate species do is intimately connected with gender identity, and in certain species, notably the chimpanzee, the gender-specific behavior that the young must learn is quite complex.

THE IMPORTANCE OF THE YOUNG AND
THE ROLES THEY PLAY

The young of any primate group provide an intense focus for all the animals in that group. As we have seen, adults and subadults, both male and female, are drawn to infants and play with them; and there is a particularly close and lasting relationship between a mother and her offspring. Juvenile females are extraordinarily interested in the young, no matter whose they are, and this interest is an important component of the learning these juveniles must do in order to become competent mothers themselves.

The intense focus upon offspring also provides a context in which adolescent males, who will eventually protect the group from predators, learn their priorities. In order to facilitate this focus, the infants of all species look rather different from adults, and ethologists see in these visual cues "releasing mechanisms" that elicit particular emotional responses from adults.

In all mammals the young of the species transmit specific signals that release cherishing behavior. These can be olfactory, acoustic, or optical, although among primates optical infant signals acquire increasing significance. Young baboons have black coats up to their sixth month. The black coat elicits help and friendly interest from the adults. Even old males will take a young baboon to clean it and help it if it is attacked. Young vervet monkeys also have a coat coloration that distinguishes them from adults. Male vervets will even attack men who lay hands on a young one with this coat. They will not, however, come to the rescue if the conspecific caught is a young vervet that has lost its baby coat. (Eibl-Eibesfeldt 1971, 123)

This extraordinary interest in the young by adult primates and the length of time this interest lasts is probably related to the extended vulnerability of primate infants. Unlike many other mammals catarrhine young reach maturity relatively slowly, and this extended maturation period is connected with the amount of learning young monkeys or apes must do in order to survive and thrive both in the natural environment and in rather complex social situations. In fact, it is probably fair to say that the primary role of the young in all higher primate societies is that of the *learner*.

THE "ATTENTION STRUCTURE" AND PRIMATE LEARNING

One way to acquire an understanding of the relationship between the learning of the young in a given primate society and the social relationships of that society is to describe the *attention structure* of the group (Chance and Jolly 1970): who pays attention to whom and why? Dominance is one important element of this attention structure in all catarrhine societies, but this importance varies according to the importance of dominance hierarchies as principles of social organization. In gorilla societies, for example,

The dominant male's behavior . . . suggests that it is designed to demand attention when, for example, by standing motionless with legs spread, he indicates his readiness to leave a nest area. . . . This fixated attention of subordinate animals would then also be the mechanism by which the dominant male determines the character of group activities. (Chance and Jolly 1970, 104)

The younger or lower-ranking males are particularly aware of what the dominant animals are doing in these societies, and explanations for this behavior emphasize the adaptive value of paying attention to dominant males (see e.g., Lorenz 1966; Wilson 1975). The dominant males of many catarrhine species are usually the most fit, in that they have the most offspring. They also bear primary responsibility for group warning and defense. Thus it probably is advantageous, in the wild, for every member of the group to pay attention to what the dominant males are doing or reacting to and learn what they have learned.

The concerns of the dominant males in a group of wild higher primates are probably crucial to the group's survival. However, the most pervasive influences in many catarrhine social groupings, as we have seen, are the relationships of the matrifocal unit, and these relationships form another significant dimension of the attention structure in any primate group. Infants watch their mothers intently at a very early age and begin to learn almost at once what is good to eat, what is dangerous, who is safe to be around, who is not to be trusted, who is a reliable playmate, and so on. As infants develop, more and more of their attention is directed outward, to a variety of foci including age-mates, subadults, dominant males, dominant females, and so forth, but it is through the complex connections rooted in the matrifocal unit that the young first learn about their world and what is expected of them in it.

The attention structure of any group of primates seems to be more complex and individualized than monitoring the behavior of dominant males and paying attention to matrifocal relationships. Kummer (1979) suggests that primate social interaction includes a kind of "feeling out" process in which the behavior of one animal is monitored by another. In the course of daily encounters — whether or not these encounters take place specifically in the context of the dominance structure or the matrifocal relations — young animals learn the subtleties of behavior of every individual in the group. By watching groups of adult males and females, by participating in a play group, and by interacting with immature siblings in the matrifocal unit, young primates are able to determine not only the rules of social behavior but how these rules might be stretched or modified depending on the individuals present. Infants learn the responses of adults and thus come to imitate as juveniles the roles they will play as mature animals.

The social environment for learning in all primate societies is exceedingly complex and demands a great deal from the young. Social competence among primates is much more than reacting to stimuli or simply following a genetic behavior program, and learning is the key to this competence. But there is no doubt in any primatologist's mind that most of the behavior one observes in wild higher primate societies is mediated by biologically based instincts—certain kinds of responses to environmental stimuli. In the next chapter I investigate these foundations of primate social life and learning.

2

The Emotional Context

THE social relationships of primate societies are mediated by emotional systems that motivate the animals to learn certain things in certain ways. Since Darwin's landmark study *The Expression of the Emotions in Man and Animals*, first published in 1872, evolutionists have known that emotional motivators of behavior (i.e., reactions, responses, expectations, etc.) are incorporated into the genetic structure of many animals, including human beings. The idea that emotional responses to stimuli from the environment (or absence of expected stimuli) represent adaptations within the species rather than simple "stimulus-response" relationships in individuals is generally accepted by those who are familiar with the principles of evolution (if not by all psychologists), but what these responses are in detail, how powerful they may be in affecting behavior, or how they may interact with an individual's learning are questions that are only beginning to be investigated.

In all higher animals there are strong internal motivations surrounding reproduction, the perception of threat, the protection of the young, and the maintenance of status or territory. When the male stickleback is mating, for example, it will attack any red object—no matter what shape or size—because during mating season the underside of male sticklebacks becomes red. The fish is thus protecting its territory from potential rivals when it attacks the color red (Tinbergen 1953). Of course, no one knows what a stickleback "feels" when it "sees red," but it is assumed that some motivational system akin to what humans identify as emotion is at work in the fish (Eibl-Eibesfeldt 1971). In many animals, especially mammals and birds, there are also particularly strong internal motivations associated with the care of the young.

Emotional systems are older than intellectual systems, for they are mediated by the *limbic system*, the area of the brain underlying the neocortex and including the thalamus, hippocampus, amygdala, and the pituitary gland. In MacLean's model of the "triune brain" (1973), the limbic system developed in the course of evolutionary processes that elaborated primitive responses to threat, hierarchy, and reproduction generated in the *R-complex* (the hindbrain) into more complicated emotional systems. The reptiles, for which the R-complex is named, had no need for sophisticated emotions, but the limbic system mediated activities that contributed to the survival of increasingly complex *social* animals. The neocortex, according to MacLean, is a more recent addition to the brain and is identified with the rise of higher mammals.

A mosquito need not learn much in order to survive long enough to fulfill its reproductive mission, but the young of many species, and particularly the primates, must learn a great deal in order to survive and thrive: "It is remarkable that some expressions of emotion which are certainly innate, require practice in the individual before they are performed in a full and perfect manner" (Darwin [1872] 1965, 351).

Few would argue that biologically based responses are associated with the care of the young in mountain gorilla mothers, but there is plenty of evidence that, in order for gorillas to become competent mothers, they must *learn* the specific skills of motherhood. Vervet monkeys (Lancaster 1971) also have a lot to learn about motherhood, as do chimpanzees (van Lawick-Goodall 1971) and, to a lesser extent, rhesus macaques (Harlow and Harlow 1965). Juvenile females are motivated to be interested in and close to the offspring of other females, form close bonds with their own offspring when they become mothers, protect them from harm, and so forth. The evidence indicates that, before the activities associated with these generalized urgings can be completed in a "full and perfect manner," they must become focused by what the monkey or ape *learns* about the rearing of the young.

We thus might say that learning serves to refine, extend, or complete activities that are originally motivated by biologically based emotional systems. But learning is itself an emotional experience. The organism is motivated to explore. Young monkeys and apes derive considerable pleasure from investigating their environment, from playing and imitating adults.

Emotional responses are largely cued by events in the environment. To use the example of the primate mothers above, the emotions of care and concern are *released* by the presence or absence of the young in a given monkey or ape group, by the presence or absence of threat, and so on. Learning, a process mediated by genetically based emotional systems, may thus extend or complete activities motivated by other emotional systems, which may in turn have been called forth by particular characteristics of the environment.

This description of the interrelationship of learning, genetically based emotional systems, and the environment is admittedly highly stylized. The interaction is incredibly subtle—particularly in higher primates, for whom learning makes significant modification of the environment possible.

What is inherited [in higher primates] is ease of learning rather than fixed instinctive patterns. The species easily, almost inevitably, learns the essential behaviors for its survival. So although it is true that monkeys learn to be social, they are so constructed that under normal circumstances this learning always takes place. Similarly human beings learn to talk, but they inherit structures that make this inevitable, except under the most peculiar circumstances. (Washburn and Hamburg 1965, 5–6)

Part of a monkey's construction, so to speak, is in emotional systems that reward the activities of learning directly. Other parts are emotional systems that are associated with successful social living. As noted in chapter 1, the social environment is a large part of the form and content of learning among all primates. Much of what young primates must learn is determined by their relations with other animals in a fairly well-defined social group, and the social environment also provides the cues for these emotional responses. The responses and the environmental cues have developed in conjunction with each other in the course of primate evolution. The characteristics of a particular primate social environment allow and encourage certain activities of learning among the young. These activities are motivated by emotional systems connected directly with the learning processes themselves and by other, deeply rooted emotional systems that motivate social behavior generally. The primate social environment reflects the existence of these emotional systems but also, in a reciprocal relationship, calls them forth. Young primates are thus motivated to learn *as social beings*.

The kinds of relationships in higher primate groups described in chapter 1 are important dimensions of social reality because evolution has produced in these animals a particular range of responses, tolerances, urges, and expectations to particular social and physiological cues. This is not to say that the behavior of catarrhines is programmed in the genes in the sense that individuals may behave in only one predetermined way. Changes in the external environment cause behavioral adaptations in individuals, and learning enables the animals in all higher primate groups to complete or fulfill activities motivated by emotions and to explore the limits of these emotions.

A number of emotional systems underlie primate social relationships. Some of the most fundamental, such as the drive to reproduce and the perception of threat, are present in the most primitive animals. But higher primate societies are diversified and complex, and learning plays a significant role in sociality. Such learning takes place in a dynamic balance in which animals are motivated both to be members of the group, willing to do whatever is necessary to remain group members, and to seek individual identity in the context of the group. The "active organism," described by Piaget, is drawn to seek experience in the social environment. It explores the oscillations of collective need and individual need and gradually learns how to be a competent adult.

A central hypothesis of this book is that three major emotional systems are intimately connected with both primate and human learning:

The emotions of attachment, belonging, and security
The emotions of individual identity and status
The emotions of investigation and discovery

It is important to mention here that, although these systems of response, expectation, and motivation may be separated for the purpose of analysis, they function all together, interacting according to the situation presented by the social or physical environment.

Washburn and DeVore (1961) describe the survival value of baboon group living:

> When the troop moves out on the daily round, *all* members must move with it, or be deserted. We have seen sick and wounded animals making great effort to keep up with the troop, and finally falling behind. At least three of these were killed, and the only protection for a baboon is to stay with the troop, no matter how injured or sick. In wild primates injuries are common . . . and animals which are so sick that they can be spotted by a relatively distant human observer are frequent. For a wild primate, a fatal sickness is one which separates it from the troop. (Quoted in Hamburg 1963, 253–54)

The feelings that connect animals to the group, urging them to keep up, are basic to individual survival; they are elaborated far beyond simple fear for personal safety, however, and are apparent in binding processes that occur in all kinds of primate social relationships.

The emotional systems connected with dominance and hierarchy play a fundamental role in status and place relations, of course, but they also provide motivations to protect the group and thus serve as binding agents. Both males and females rush to protect the young, and as mentioned in chapter 1, the physical characteristics of infants are releasing mechanisms that elicit highly emotional responses in adults in certain situations. Van Lawick-Goodall (1971) reports that, on several occasions when the chimpanzee troop she was observing began to hunt young baboons, male baboons appeared almost immediately and engaged in aggressive (though bloodless) tussles with the male chimps. Most of the time, the young baboons escaped in the confusion.

These impulses to protect the young offer the great benefit of security. This security is vital to the learning of the young because it allows them the unencumbered time and confidence to experiment, to practice and refine skills, and to explore the world around them.

Most prominent in terms of the emotional systems of attachment, belonging, and security are the relations that surround the matrifocal unit. Many have noted the intensely emotional state of infants separated from their mothers, the corresponding distress of mothers separated from their offspring, and the powerful attraction that infants have for all females of any primate group. These emotional attachments are extended, to some degree, throughout matrifocal units or genealogies as the infant grows, but a singular emotional connection with the mother remains well into adulthood. The evidence suggests that, when coalitions among primates form, they develop in terms of matrifocal relationships, and no doubt these agreements are made possible by emotional attachments formed in the context of the matrifocal unit.

The emotions surrounding reproduction draw males and females to one another during female estrus, and this attraction reflects powerful biological responses to internal and visual cues. The estrus swelling of the female in all primate species (except humans) is a releasing mechanism that sets off mating behavior in even infant males (van Lawick-Goodall 1971). As we have seen, however, within the context of these overwhelming motivations, other, individual attachments may develop. Even though such attachments appear to exist only in the context of female estrus, they, like the more fundamental attachments of reproduction, bind animals together into a social group.

Finally, emotional connections develop among *individuals* in a group. There are no neutral observers in a primate society; every animal, whether infant, dominant female, or adolescent male, is a participant and is familiar with every other animal in the group. Though the emotional connections between individuals formed in play or in grooming may be considered variations on the more imperative emotional systems that bind animals together, there is little doubt that they too contribute to the group's coherence and thus to the learning of the young.

INDIVIDUAL IDENTITY AND STATUS

Coexistent and, to a certain extent, conflicting with the emotions that bind group members together and motivate them to seek and provide security and stability are the emotions that urge individuals to define their identity in the group and protect their individual status. These emotions are most obvious in primate males, but within the matrifocal dimension of social experience, females are also engaged in determining their identity and are quite capable of protecting their status.

It is hard to know what the chimpanzee Mike was feeling as he watched the dominant males grooming one another, but van Lawick-Goodall makes it clear that this moment was intensely emotional for him. It is interesting that he did not actually have to fight the other males in his drive to define his personal status. The commotion he made with the kerosene cans was enough to establish some sort of individuality, which became translated into status. It is equally hard to know what the dominant males felt as Mike made his charge with the cans. Surely they were afraid, but it is likely that this was not the same sort of fear they would have felt at the approach of a leopard.

The intricacies of dominance and status relationships among primates of different species are little known, but it is probably safe to say that every animal in a primate group is engaged in the determination—that is to say, the *discovery*—of individual place in relationship to other animals. That this is neither a simple nor a linear determination is clear from the variety of behaviors exhibited by dominant animals toward other animals in the group. Mountain gorilla silverbacks and chimpanzees are remarkably tolerant of infants but are less tolerant of juveniles. Van Lawick-Goodall noted that, once the kerosene can-banging Mike secured his position as dominant male of the chimpanzee group, he frequently shared meat with other animals.

A great deal of a young primate's identity is formed and discovered in the play group in which the young try out adult behavior oriented to the determination of status (see below). While it is impossible to assess in detail all the ways in which aggressive play is mediated by emotional responses, there is no doubt that play activity is highly charged with feeling.

INVESTIGATION AND DISCOVERY

The young of all primate groups appear to be motivated internally to seek experience in their world. They establish contact with the external environment early on through observation and later, through investigative behavior and play, explore the physical and social dimensions available to them (see chapter 3). Not only are primate young emotionally stimulated to investigate, they also apparently derive pleasure from novel discoveries and are motivated to seek further novelty.

> It is the young who still have the greatest amount of untapped novelty to explore and who are more frequently reinforced by novelty reinforcers for further exploration, play, and creativity. Hence, younger primates tend to generate a higher frequency of the explorative and playful behavior which may lead to useful innovations. The habits of exploration, play and creativity tend to be extinguished and replaced by less variable routines by middle or late adulthood. (Baldwin and Baldwin 1979, 103)

Here are echoes of Piaget (see e.g., 1952), who saw all living things as active organisms, internally motivated to interact with their environments. Another way of describing the gradual reduction of the explorative and playful behavior might be, in Piaget's terms, the "gradual achievement of equilibrium."

Harlow and Mears (1979) provide ample evidence of the persistence of curiosity displayed by all primates. The learning activities of observation, imitation, exploration, and, above all, play are pleasurable and exciting for young primates. This connection reveals a key evolutionary process. The arousal, excitement, and pleasure encourage the young primate to engage in activities through which it will learn what is necessary to survive and thrive in both the physical and social environments.

Young primates learn, as they grow and mature, how to be members of their group. Being a member of the group implies sexuality, protection and care of the young, involvement in status structures, and many more intricate relationships that are set in the context of reproduction, dominance, and the matrifocal unit. The various activities of learning—observation, exploration, and play—have developed as integral elements of this process. Youngsters are bound to the group through innate emotional responses and through the activities they engage in as they mature. What is learned and the ways in which it is learned are not separable in primate societies, for the time and energy spent in play and exploration result in group-living adults who competently fulfill the roles that contribute to the survival and well-being of the group and to their individual status and well-being as well. Young primates "learn inevitably" how to function in the physical environment and in their societies at least in part because such learning is mediated by emotional systems that ensure a secure environment for the activities of learning, help create the social context in which these activities take place, and reward these learning activities directly.

3

How Primates Learn

THE young of all primate species learn by doing—by observing, by trying out their observations (imitating) and testing their abilities in play, and by purposefully investigating the environment in which they live. Shortly after the reflex period of infant development, catarrhine young begin to look around, first observing their mothers' behavior, then widening their attention to include other members of the group. They begin to focus more intently on environmental events and the activities of others. But do catarrhines actually *learn* by this observation?

Butler offers an account of an experiment by Darby and Riopelle in 1959 that demonstrated unequivocally that they do.

In their experiment, one rhesus monkey observed another perform a long series of two-choice visual discrimination problems for food reward. The demonstrator would make a choice, the discriminanda would be returned to their original positions, and then the observer would be permitted to respond. The performance of the observer improved as the experiment progressed. What is exciting about this experiment is that the observer obtained more information about a particular problem when the demonstrator made an incorrect response than when it responded correctly. This means that the observing monkey was not merely repeating the acts of the demonstrator; it was responding to the consequences of the demonstrator's behavior. (Butler 1965, 490–91)

It thus appears that, not only are catarrhines able to learn from observing the behavior of other animals, they are able to interpret mistakes and inconsistencies in this behavior and modify their own accordingly.

But the primate infant is far from a passive observer. From birth it has engaged in a strong physical and emotional interaction with its mother, and as it grows it extends this interaction to other members of the group and to the external environment. Young primates *play* ("Indeed, when young chimpanzees are two or three years old it often seems that they do little else" [van Lawick-Goodall 1971, 163]). Through the activities of play the young of all catarrhine species learn much of what they need to know in order to survive and be competent group members.

> Play repertoires of young monkeys contain the origins of most adult social behaviors. Patterns of social grooming, dominance, aggression, and sex are clearly evident in monkey play activity, though not at competent adult levels. At first clumsy to the point of being ridiculous, months and even years of practice at play produce the adult product. (Harlow and Mears 1979, 145–46)

Field evidence (Dolhinow and Bishop 1970; van Lawick-Goodall 1965, 1971) corroborates the laboratory observations that play includes segments of adult behavior that the young are trying out. Play is an endless repetition of roughhouse, mounting, and aggressive display, in all possible combinations.

Imitating adults in play allows young primates to discover adult behavior as they mature. From fragments of behavior, jumbled and out of context in infancy, adolescents begin to string together appropriate adult repertoires, even as they become physically capable of engaging in them as young adults. Through observation and in play youngsters come to understand something about the contexts in which these adult behaviors have meaning: dominance and hierarchy, mating, grooming, and so forth. They thus master not only the behavior required of them but the meaning and appropriateness of this behavior as well.

There is no need for instruction of the young by the adults because the activities of learning, the physical maturation of the young, and the content that needs to be learned are all perfectly integrated. Young primates are genetically endowed with an emotional system that rewards exploration and discovery, and this system motivates them to interact with and press the limits of their environment—both physical and social. All a young primate needs to learn is before it from birth. Adults are ever-present, and their behavior is always observable. Subsistence techniques, dominance relations, the connections of the matrifocal unit, male-female relations, and the treatment of the young are immediately obvious to learning primates, who can then take bits and snatches of what they see into the play group to try out. Because the adults in higher primate societies assure the young of a relatively secure environment, the individuals in a play group are able to practice behavior and specific skills for a long time (compared with the amount of practice time available to mammals other than humans) before being called upon to function as adults, and they have the confidence to take greater risks than most other mammals in their explorations. Finally, the crucial relationships that individual animals develop with other individuals are formed in play.

The long-term studies made at the Japanese Monkey Center (see Itani 1958) offer a remarkable example of how learning occurs in a primate society and how information is disseminated through the attention structure of the group and the activities of play. In 1952, researchers studying Japanese macaque behavior on Koshima Island threw sweet potatoes on a sandy beach. Although the monkeys were fond of the potatoes, they were bothered by the gritty beach sand, which they tried to brush off. About a year after the potatoes first appeared, a juvenile female (one and one-half years old) acquired the habit of washing her potatoes in the sea before eating them.

The observers traced the spread of this innovation carefully. The first animal to learn the potato-washing trait from the juvenile who invented it was her mother.

This is understandable, since practically the only adult animal to be interested in the behavior of a one-and-one-half-year-old female is her mother. Once the mother had adopted the behavior then it passed naturally to all her subsequent offspring. An older sibling of the juvenile innovator learned the behavior several years later, probably from watching her young sister. The main line of diffusion of sweet potato washing was through the play group of the young female. Some of her playmates were interested in her behavior, observed the potato washing, and began doing it themselves. Their mothers and older siblings then learned it and so the habit passed through other genealogies. Eventually, through the attention structures of the matrifocal units and the play group all but 13 monkeys (mostly adult males) had learned to wash potatoes. The adult males were not resistant to the idea on principle; they simply did not notice what was going on in a way that would affect their behavior. (Lancaster 1975, 45–46)

Some time after sweet potatoes were introduced, piles of wheat were dumped on the same beach, and the *same female* discovered a way to remove the sand by sluicing handfuls of the wheat into pools of water. The wheat floated, the sand sank, and the animal could eat by simply skimming the wheat off the water. Interestingly enough, this innovation also took years to spread through the group. After three years only fourteen out of fifty-eight animals had learned the new technique. By contrast, when wheat was given to another monkey group in which the only animal familiar with the new food (and also familiar with the sluicing technique) was a dominant male, the innovation spread through the group—from the male to other dominant males, then to the dominant females and, from there, through the dominance and matrifocal pathways to all the animals in the group—within a matter of *hours* (Kawai 1965).

The "monkey genius" of Koshima Island at no time engaged her peers or her mother in ways that might be interepreted as demonstration behavior. She did not show them how it was done, and at all times the responsibility for learning the new technique and modifying their own behavior accordingly rested solely with the observers.

In this example we may catch a glimpse of the complexity of primate social organization and its relationship to learning. The importance of dominance and dominance hierarchies to the attention structure of this group of macaques is demonstrated by the rapid diffusion of the wheat-sluicing technique through a group of monkeys when the innovator was a dominant male. At the same time, what might be called the conservative nature of dominance hierarchies may be supposed from the inability of the adult males in the original group to pay attention to the sweet-potato washing technique, even though it was advantageous for them to do so. One might assume that a general lack of interest on the part of all adults would be related to the replacement of novelty with established routines noted by the Baldwins. On the basis of the Koshima example, however, dominance hierarchies seem to affect the attention structure of the group in such a way that information can flow through them only in one direction—from top to bottom. Only very gradually does information work its way from bottom to top.

As we have seen, such an arrangement is probably adaptive for the group,* and it is important to note that there was no *resistance* to the new technique on the part of the adult males who did not pick it up. They did not view the technique as a threat to their status and attempt to suppress it. Indeed, there is a good deal of evidence to suggest that dominance hierarchies are somewhat self-contained dimensions of primate social interaction that may remain relatively unaffected by interactions in other dimensions. Lancaster (1975) reports that, when coalitions of female vervet monkeys chase males away from infants, the males' status in their dominance hierarchy is unchanged. Van Lawick-Goodall reports that the presence of meat in a chimpanzee group may temporarily alter the workings of the dominance structure, but the overall status of individual animals is unaffected by these events.

The other great dimension of primate social organization is the matrifocal unit, and in the Koshima example we see that, although the interactions in this dimension seem to be more subtle and long-term, they are no less important. The stability of the matrifocal genealogies in macaque groups suggests a different sort of conservatism at work in these societies. The status of these genealogies may remain relatively the same for long periods of time, but it appears that matrifocal relations admit a two-way

---

*The arrangement is adaptive for a *thoroughly* wild group, isolated from humans. An interesting case could be made that one of the reasons gorilla societies are in such decline is that the male-dominance network is as conservative and inflexible as it is. In the wild these dominance structures are well adapted to the demands of survival, but when gorillas come in contact with human beings, flexibility and the capacity to expand the attention structure are crucial to survival. The chimpanzee attention structure is more flexible than the gorilla structure, and chimpanzees are thus able to adapt more easily to unfamiliar environments.

flow of information. The mother of the juvenile female innovator was the first animal to learn the new technique, and all her subsequent offspring learned to wash potatoes from watching and imitating her. The next animal to learn the potato-washing technique was the innovator's older sister (a sibling in the matrifocal unit), who also learned the technique by observing and imitating her younger sister and/or her mother. Finally, the importance of play as a learning activity is demonstrated in this example, for the potato-washing technique was diffused through the play group within which the younger macaques were able to pay close attention to one another and experiment.

Potato-washing and wheat sluicing are simple tasks for higher primates to learn (if they are able to pay attention), but the social skills connected with complex relationships between animals in the context of their need to be part of the group and their simultaneous need to acquire personal identity and status require much practice and investigation before they are mastered. In the rise of Mike the chimpanzee, described in chapter 1, one may catch a glimpse of how both these needs may be addressed in a primate society. Mike's drive to acquire status led him to disrupt the group of peacefully grooming males with his crashing kerosene cans. Later, when he had achieved status, his meat-sharing activities served to bring the group members closer together and bound him to them.

The learning of all primates occurs in a dynamic balance between the need to belong to the group and the need to acquire personal identity and status. In dominance relationships between males and between females, both needs may be addressed. An individual animal that seeks identity and status also accepts responsibility for the protection of the young or of the entire group. Though matrifocal units provide a fundamental sense of attachment and closeness for the animals involved, they also have a significant effect on an individual's status in the whole group. The reproductive urges during female estrus tie animals in the group together, of course, but so does the intense focus on the young. And the security that this adult concern generates enables the young to be confident enough to take risks as they learn how to acquire individual identity and status.

As the upright primate of four million years ago evolved into a hominid and thence into a human, the dimensions of social experience were greatly expanded, but the underlying emotional systems remained and guided the social developments of our ancestors. Throughout all that history, until very recent times, the content and processes of learning were one and the same. The activities through which young hominids acquired information about the physical environment, the skills of subsistence, and their social relations were activities that bound them to one another and also allowed them to establish individual identities. These activities were so emotionally charged (with pleasure, fear, arousal, and excitement) that young hominids, like young contemporary primates, sought out these kinds of experiences until they had exhausted the possibilities. In the next chapter we shall see how the social possibilities (and thus the learning demands and possibilities) expanded for early humans.

Part 2

The Human Adaptation

4

The Emergence of Human Society

SOMETIME during the Pliocene, between four and five million years ago, new primates emerged in East Africa—ground-dwelling animals that walked upright. These creatures were our ancestors, and as they evolved they built upon the old primate social relations increasingly complex and distinctly human adaptations.

The hard evidence for ancient hominids—the stones and bones—is unfortunately sparse, and although this deficiency has not deterred archaeologists and others from forming hypotheses on the basis of the artifacts that have been uncovered, the dearth of hard evidence has always left such ideas open to charges of unwarranted speculation. Interpreters of archaeological material have so little to work with that they must use other frames of reference, such as primate studies and the ethnographic literature on foraging societies, in which paleolithic hominid and human bones and stone tools can be located. The occasions for error in such a situation are many, of course, and have been pointed out many times (e.g., in Lee and DeVore 1968; Wobst 1978). Nevertheless, faced with the choice between making interpretations that are plausible (given the available evidence) but unprovable (until further evidence is discovered) and withholding all interpretation, students of human evolution seem compelled to take the risk of the former alternative. I am no exception, because the links between what has been learned from studying other primates and the behavior of modern humans may be forged only through an interpretation of the archaeological record.

Not only is this work sketchy, it is fraught with political pitfalls as well. Just as evolutionary biology has at times become polarized by the possibility of unpleasant extensions of theories concerning the genetic basis for behavior, models of human evolution built on archaeological evidence may become polarized by extensions of the meanings of artifacts. For example, the longer a characteristic of human behavior or social organization has existed in the hominid family, the more "respectability" it has as an adaptation of the species. Bipedalism is an ancient hominid characteristic. The fossil evidence indicates that a physiological adaptation for an upright posture is at least four million years old. But if bipedalism, which we know is ancient, is closely connected with the development of the human nuclear family, uniquely human sexual behavior, and the sexual division of labor (as it is in Lovejoy 1981), the interpretation acquires political significance. The meaning of gender roles and family relations is giving us lots of trouble today. To add to the confusion, there have been a number of popularizations of human evolution and our relationship to our primate cousins (e.g., Ardrey 1966; Morris 1967) and even "historical" novels (e.g., Auel 1980) about what our ancestors must have thought and felt.

The variables in human evolution are bewilderingly complex. Sometime between one and five million years ago, a number of significant changes occurred in groups of primates living in East Africa: they became bipedal, used and made tools more purposefully than their ancestors had, began to eat larger game, and utilized home bases. The males and females of these groups evolved a complementary division of labor that included the regular sharing of food. Female estrus disappeared, males became bonded to the primary matrifocal unit, and these families came to constitute the primary units of human society. The offspring of these animals were born at an earlier state of development than were the young of other primates and consequently had a longer period of maturation—which insured a greater capacity for learning. Finally, this line developed a large and complex brain.

Many of these attributes may have been prefigured in earlier primate societies in which the animals hunted or scavenged, had developed certain specializations of activity according to gender, and made and used tools of one sort or another. But what catapulted these new primates into unique areas of behavioral and social complexity, how extensions of primate characteristics became differentiated into qualitatively different human characteristics, and how these characteristics affected one another's development are extraordinarily difficult questions. That we are related to these creatures is assumed by all (as it is assumed that we are related to chimpanzees), but the ways in which that relatedness is reflected in our own behavior will always be open to speculation.

Although paleoanthropologists disagree about how many species of hominids existed between one and four million years ago, there is evidence that, by about two million years ago, some hominids were using stone tools to butcher large animals and were transporting tool materials and meat to what might have been base camps. The social understanding and skill required of a member of such a society was much greater than had been necessary for competence in earlier primate groups, and the young therefore had a great deal more to learn.

It is safe to assume that becoming competent in social relations as a member of a group was an even more important function of learning for young, group-living hominids than it is for contemporary social primates because the most significant growth in the brain during hominid development took place in areas that are associated with social life.

> We saw during the last 2.3 million years of hominid evolution almost a tripling in brain size, most of which can be attributed to the massive growth of the neocortex. This growth, however, was not equivalent in all regions of the brain; rather it was disproportionately greater in the regions which mediate the psychological functions identified as "social competency." (Fishbein 1979, 207–8)

The human brain evolved in a *matrix* of social and biological developments. Brain complexity and social complexity became linked in coevolution. The young of these advanced hominids, or early humans, were capable of learning more and more — and there was more and more to learn.

THE ELEMENTS OF EARLY HUMAN SOCIETY

We may never know with any certainty when or how the distinctly human social adaptations emerged, but it is important to see that these adapta-

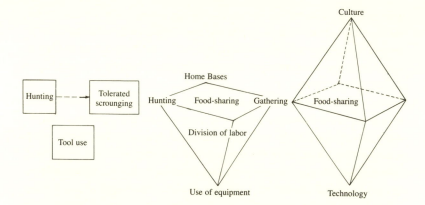

Behavior patterns that differ in degree of organization are contrasted in these diagrams. Living great apes, exemplified here by the chimpanzee, exhibit behavior patterns that became important in human evolution but the patterns (*left*) exist largely as isolated elements. Hunting occurs on a small scale but leads only to "tolerated scrounging" rather than active food-sharing; similarly, tools are used but tool use is not integrated with hunting or scrounging. The author's model (*center*) integrates these three behavior patterns and others into a coherent structure. Food-sharing is seen as a central structural element, incorporating the provision of both animal and plant foods, the organization of a home base and a division of labor. Supporting the integrated structure is a necessary infrastructure of tool and equipment manufacture; for example, without devices for carrying foodstuffs there could not be a division of labor and organized food-sharing. In modern human societies (*right*) the food-sharing structure has undergone socioeconomic elaboration. Its infrastructure now incorporates all of technology, and a matching superstructure has arisen to incorporate other elements of what is collectively called culture. From "The Food-Sharing Behavior of Protohuman Hominids" by Glynn Issac. Copyright © 1978 by Scientific American, Inc. All rights reserved.

tions were *cooperative* in nature. They were characterized by *reciprocal arrangements* new to the primate order. At the same time, they continued to reflect the ancient balance between collective and individual needs. Glynn Isaac (1978) has proposed a model for such arrangements on the basis of evidence from several sites around Koobi Fora in East Africa. Isaac no longer believes that the Koobi Fora finds prove that the hominids living there two million years ago used home bases. But I think that his Food-Sharing Hypothesis serves as an excellent model to illustrate the complexity of the matrix within which modern humans ultimately evolved, whenever these characteristics first emerged.

Isaac presents a model of human evolution in which the division of labor and the utilization of home bases interact in a flexible feedback relationship with the use of equipment and tools and the sharing of food. Innovation or change in one area of activity or relationship would affect every other area, and these effects would trigger others. (See figure on page 58.)

Food sharing and the division of labor were significant elements of the social environment in which the young grew and learned, and the complexity generated by such social relationships required increasingly more learning. It is likely that the principles of reciprocity, the bonds of kinship, and the importance of gender identity in the acquisition of particular skills and knowledge have been central to hominid and human learning for at least one million years.

We may suppose that dominance (in both male-male and female-female relations), matrifocal connections, rudimentary specializations of activity by sex, and a significant focus on the young characterized the primates of East Africa before the development of the hominids. These social relationships formed the basis from which early human relationships were elaborated. As these human social relationships became more complex, the attention structure of the group widened to include more adults of both sexes, gender identity became more complicated and more intimately associated with subsistence, and the young took on an even more important function in the group.

DOMINANCE AND HIERARCHY

The character of dominance relationships began to change toward *less* emphasis on hierarchy with the evolution of distinctly hominid characteristics. The most important component of this change in dominance was the attachment of the male to a mother and her offspring to form the human family as the primary unit of social life. In some imprecise period of time a veritable cascade of interconnected characteristics associated with this unique primate adaptation evolved. The sexual divison of labor, food sharing, reciprocal obligation, and the loss of female estrus all imply the gradual development of a kind of partnership between adult males and females that extended beyond the urgencies of reproduction (Lancaster 1975).

One of the most profound effects of the evolution of the human family on the learning of the young was a reordering and complication of the attention structure within the group. As noted in chapter 1, the dominant males and the mothers in all primate societies are major foci for the attention of other animals in the group. But in a society that consisted of a number of family units, the attention of the young would be primarily focused not on single males or on mothers but on *parents* in the family unit and, ultimately, on an array of related adults. An important implication of this shift is that a more flexible, more responsive attention structure evolved in which animals paid attention to and were interested in the behavior of an increasingly wider range of individuals. One interesting result of this expansion of the attention structure might have been that innovations discovered by younger animals had a better chance of passing through a group of hominids quickly, making the group more immediately responsive to environmental fluctuations. It is only speculation, of course, but one supposes that a subsistence technique invented by a juvenile female in a hominid group would have been adopted by the whole group far more rapidly than was sweet-potato washing in a twentieth-century macaque troop.

Another result of this collaboration between the male and female dominance structures was that there were many more opportunities for individual animals to acquire identity and status in the group. Males and females could be recognized as individuals within their own families, whatever their status in the larger society. A third result of this change in dominance patterns was no doubt an exponential leap in the complexity of the identity and status relationships the young had to learn about.

MALE-FEMALE RELATIONS AND ROLES

The rapidly evolving early humans that lived from 500,000 to 1,000,000 years ago expanded the rudimentary gender specializations of earlier primates into a totally new system of social organization. For the first time in primate history, deep and reciprocal bonds developed between adult males and females. The loss of estrus has been interpreted as evidence of selection for this bonding (Ullock and Wagner 1980; Van Den Berghe 1979, 1980). In this interpretation sex became such an important component of the bond that females with longer or more frequent periods of sexual receptivity and males who were more sociable with females during and beyond these periods of receptivity were more successful in reproducing than animals without these traits. The overwhelming drives surrounding reproduction in other primates (absent when females are not in estrus) became generalized human behavior, contributing not only to the survival of the species but to the binding of individuals together as husband/father and wife/mother.

The sexual division of labor that evolved in the context of these bonds formed a new and marvelously efficient subsistence strategy. We have seen that there are some gender-role specializations in every higher primate society and that in some (notably the chimpanzee) there is specialization of activity with regard to subsistence. But perhaps as many as one million years ago, this role specialization became the central theme of survival. Males and females each contributed to the survival of the family and to the whole group by procuring different kinds of foods. The foods obtained by females could be *gathered*, that is, obtained close to the home base so that the young could be carried along. The foods obtained by males were *hunted* and drew the males away from the home base for days at a time. The arrangement thus allowed for adequate child care and the procurement of a wide variety of foods.

Out of this arrangement evolved increasingly elaborate systems of reciprocity that included the kin of both the male and the female in the family. These complex reciprocal alliances, expectations, and conventions formed another large part of the new content the young had to learn.

The details of the development of the human division of labor will forever be unknown, but it is clear that a relationship evolved between the extension and refinement of gender roles and the opportunities these roles offered for sharing, cooperation, and reciprocity. In this way further separation of roles by sex brought animals closer together and thus contributed to the emergence of the family and kin as primary social learning environments.

THE YOUNG

With the appearance of the family structure among early humans, the importance of the young in the society acquired new dimensions. Reciprocal attachments were formed between fathers and their offspring that no doubt enhanced the survival chances of the young because the father's concern for *individual* offspring (as opposed to the generalized fatherhood of the primates noted in chapter 1) increased access to food and extended the security within which the young could learn.

In the context of father-child and other family attachments, the young became *shared* foci of attention for males and females, and this shared focus drew husband and wife and all their kin more closely together. It is likely that the importance of infants, shared by all primate societies, did not disappear as infants became adolescents. Juveniles in higher primate societies are usually ignored by adults, but in a system of family and kin connections, adolescents would have *increased* importance as they approached marriage.

No doubt the learner role of the young, a feature common to all primate societies, became increasingly important, even crucial, to the survival and well-being of the young in these early human societies. These infants were born at an earlier stage of development than other primates and were thus more vulnerable for a longer period of time. The family structure provided the greater security needed for these neonates to mature and learn properly, supplied the attention structure through which the young learned, and also provided models of complex social behavior and physical skill.

But if the social environment for learning changed, there is no reason to believe that learning took place in activities other than those practiced by other primate young. It is more likely that the activities of primate learning—observation, imitation, exploration, play—were *intensified* in the course of hominid evolution, for they could be engaged in for increasingly longer stretches of immaturity and were stimulated by an increasingly complex variety of social interactions represented by the sexual division of labor, kinship, food sharing, tool and equipment manufacture and use, and reciprocal obligation. With the evolution of language and complex material cultures, the early human societies became even more efficient at survival through the great advantage of more sophisticated communication. In addition, language and culture further reinforced the bonds among group members and, at some point, enabled the idea of the group to emerge (see chapter 12). No doubt the young of *Homo erectus* 500,000 years ago "learned inevitably" how to become competent members of the group they were part of, in the environment they lived in; by this time, however, the complexity of the human learning process, if not the effort of it, was astounding.

THE FORAGING WAY OF LIFE

Sometime during the existence of *Homo erectus*, if not before, our ancestors became hunters and gatherers. The fact that the hunting-and-gathering way of life has persisted into modern times in many parts of the world affords us an opportunity to understand the social complexity that developed in early human societies and the relationship these societies had with the physical environment.

As with studies of other primate groups and interpretations of archaeological evidence, the examination of contemporary hunting and gathering societies for the light they may shed on our hominid or early human ancestors is problematic. Anthropology itself is a relatively new discipline that grew haphazardly from the observations of Western travelers in different parts of the world. The first anthropologists attempted to bring order to their observations and to integrate them into large-scale theories of human social organization. From the formal beginnings of the discipline in the late nineteenth century, many anthropologists have operated under the assumption that the so-called primitive societies of the world reflect an earlier state of human social development—though there has been little agreement about the meaning of such a statement.

From the perspective of the late nineteenth and early twentieth century heyday of the industrial revolution, in which anthropology was born, it was probably impossible for anthropologists to conceive of nomadic foraging peoples as anything but curious carryovers from the Stone Age. These people, after all, were the *most* primitive from the perspective of technological development and manipulation of the external environment. They had somehow been missed by civilization and were inferior because of it. They had not progressed, and the theories of human social organization that emerged from the study of band societies with minimal technology often reflect these essentially Western, progress- and property-oriented assumptions.

The assumptions of anthropologists concerning so-called primitive

societies have undergone wholesale revision in the last twenty five years.*
In the context of an evolutionary perspective—often missing in the work
of early anthropologists but present in some recent ethnographic work—
nomadic foraging societies have come to be viewed not as isolated groups
that "time forgot" but as representatives of a remarkably successful,
stable, and persistent human adaptation that cuts across tremendous environmental variation.

I am not saying that contemporary gatherers and hunters are "Stone
Age remnants" or that they are in any way less human than any other
representatives of the species, but only that the nomadic foraging way
of life is the ancient framework for human subsistence and social organization within which evolved our capacities, abilities, emotional systems,
and social relationships. It is now clear that life in nomadic foraging
societies is neither nasty nor brutish. In fact, because of the relatively
small amount of time and effort devoted to subsistence and the great
amount of leisure available to all, Marshall Sahlins (1968) has called
gathering-and-hunting groups the "original affluent society."

Life in nomadic foraging societies is full of the same kinds of human
urgencies, satisfactions, betrayals, and complexities that characterize
any human group. Of course, these highly charged activities are played
out in different ways, in response to different environmental pressures.
But the *kinds* of social interactions that people in gathering-and-hunting
societies respond to with intensity, animation, and concern are the same
kinds of social interactions that command the attention of us all.

The gathering-and-hunting framework has all but disappeared from
the earth today as other, recently developed social systems have exerted
pressure upon it, but there is little doubt that this way of life was the
context in which hominids became human and we humans spent the bulk
of our evolutionary history. There is archaeological evidence that our
ancient ancestors lived this way and *no* evidence that they lived in any
other way. Though we may be sure that the nomadic foraging groups we
know about today are not the same as the nomadic foraging groups that
roamed East African savannas 500,000 years ago, it is likely that many
characteristics of the foraging way of life have remained similar.

* This revision is perhaps related to the perspective one is afforded from what might be
called the downside of the industrial revolution as well as to increasingly accurate data.

The best explanation for the similarities among these [contemporary foraging] groups is that within the gathering and hunting mode, there is a limited set of alternatives to choose from. Any group of people who had to live off the land would face similar ecological problems and would probably invent a roughly similar system. It seems reasonable to suggest, then, that this pattern—or more properly, this range of patterns—prevailed in most human societies before the agricultural revolution and during much of the course of human evolution. (Shostak 1981, 46)

The terms *nomadic foraging society, gatherers and hunters, hunter-gatherers*, and *foraging bands* are somewhat misleading, for the peoples of the earth live and probably have lived since the development of agriculture somewhere along a continuum that ranges from complete foraging and no domestication of animals to a high degree of specialization, city dwelling in large populations, and so forth. Certainly there are societies at various places on this continuum still in existence in many parts of the world today. I intend here, however, to present the framework for social relations and organization that most probably characterized hominid and human groups for as many as one million years *before* the advent of agriculture. Accordingly, the following definition has been used to characterize the nomadic foraging societies discussed in this book.

We make two basic assumptions about hunters and gatherers: (1) they live in small groups and (2) they move around a lot. Each local group is associated with a geographical range but these groups do not function as closed social systems. Probably from the very beginning there was communication between groups, including reciprocal visiting and marriage alliances, so that the basic hunting society consisted of a series of local "bands" which were part of a larger breeding and linguistic community. The economic system is based on several core features including a home base or camp, a division of labor—with males hunting and females gathering—and, most important, a pattern of sharing out the collected food resources.

These few broadly defined features provide an organizational base line of the small-scale society from which subsequent develop-

ments can be derived. We visualize a social system with the following characteristics. First, if individuals and groups have to move
around in order to get food there is an important implication: the
amount of personal property has to be kept to a very low level. . . .

Second, the nature of the food supply keeps the living groups
small, usually under fifty persons. . . .

Third, the local groups as groups do not ordinarily maintain
exclusive rights to resources. . . .

Fourth, food surpluses are not a prominent feature of the small-
scale society. . . .

Fifth, frequent visiting between resource areas prevents any one
group from becoming too strongly attached to any single area. (Lee
and DeVore 1968, 11–12)

By this definition groups such as the Northwest Coast Indians of North
America, who obtained their food primarily from fishing and hunting but
lived in large, permanently inhabited villages, would not be considered
gatherers and hunters and will not be addressed here. Neither are slash-
and-burn agriculturalists, who hunt or fish to supplement their food supply, included in this study.

Perhaps the most striking characteristic of life in nomadic foraging
societies is what might be called its wholeness, its fully integrated nature.
Every activity, from tool manufacture to healing, is connected with every
other activity. The foraging life is a great circle of social relationships
that revolve in dynamic equilibrium with the physical environment.
Wherever the student enters this circle, balances, obligations, connections, expectations, and symbols stretch around in either direction. Early
human societies probably existed in this same state of integration.

The importance of the reliance on the natural environment cannot be
overemphasized. The hunting-and-gathering life is lived in an intimate
and immediate connection with the natural environment for all life
processes. All food, all clothing, all tools, and all shelter are drawn from
materials that are available in the local environment. Changes in the
seasons, the weather, the patterns of animal migration, or water availability significantly affect the people in a foraging group, and the movements
and cycles of the Australian aborigines, the !Kung of the Kalahari, the

Eskimo, or the Mbuti Pygmies of Zaire are inextricably woven into the cycles of the desert, the arctic, and the rain forest.

In every environment in which hunting-and-gathering societies exist, a stable pattern of relationship, an ecology, has developed between the size of the subsistence group and availability of resources. Even though there may be a considerable amount of variation in the size of any particular group at any particular time, an upper limit on the size of the band is imposed by the physical environment. Bands typically consist of groups of from twenty-five to fifty people from related families that live and travel together, and there is some evidence that the average size of subsistence groups in paleolithic times fell within this range as well (Birdsell 1968).

The "average range" of 25 to 50 members of a band in no way implies a static population. The size and membership of a band fluctuate constantly. All foraging societies display a pattern of coming together and breaking apart that is closely connected with the cycles of the physical environment and the availability of resources. The !Kung break into average-sized bands throughout the wet season and come together gradually into substantially larger groups around major water holes during the dry months. The Netsilik Eskimo form caribou-hunting and salmon-fishing groups of 25 to 50 individuals for most of the year and then come together in groups that may number 150 or more for breathing-hole sealing in deep winter.

The fluctuations of the physical environment are intertwined with the social needs of hunter-gatherers. When the small groups come together around a water hole or on a winter ice floe, old relationships are renewed and new ones are begun. Marriages are contracted and relatives are revisited. It is a time for celebration and healing. The crucial social activities of these groups have developed in concert with variations in the external environment.

Another consequence of living in a direct connection with the physical environment for all life processes and materials is that there is no question about the value of one's activity. Making an arrow, digging out a root, or telling a story all have an "absolute meaning" because they are intimately connected with individual and group survival and well-being.

This fact of life in a gathering-and-hunting band is hard for people from a modern technological society to grapple with; we are separated in so many ways from the physical environment. But the absolute conviction of the worth of one's work forms the background of all learning in nomadic foraging societies. No doubt the background for the learning of the young in early human societies was similar.

The need to be connected and to belong to the group, the need to acquire individual identity and status, and the need to investigate and seek experience — the same emotional urges that create the social environment in which young primates learn and compel them to participate in the activities of learning — form the foundation of learning for the young in foraging societies. A detailed examination of learning and relationships in foraging societies will demonstrate that these same emotional systems underlie all human social interaction.

5

The Emotional Context of Learning

in Foraging Societies

CHILDREN in foraging societies know precisely what the relationship is between what they are learning and what they will be required to do as adults. This relevance in their learning is automatic because the group they belong to offers them both clear visions of adult reality and plenty of opportunity to imitate and practice the skills and behavior they witness. In these societies children know how they fit with all the other members of the group, and conventions of reciprocity tie them to family and friends. It is self-evident to them that what they learn will provide them with both membership in a community and individual identity and status.

ATTACHMENT, BELONGING, AND SECURITY

Within the security of the family and the universe of kin and in the daily presence of conventions of reciprocity, conversation, and ceremony, children grow and learn. From the moment of birth, infants spend almost all their time in direct physical contact with their mothers. Whether babies are carried in the *amaut* of the Inuit or the *kaross* of the !Kung, they ride in warmth and safety, always close to the breast. Even toddlers are frequently carried by their mothers until they are weaned to make way for a new sibling, and this intense, long-term contact engenders deep and lasting bonds between mothers and their children, both male and female (see e.g., Konner 1976).

The mothers have the primary responsibility for infant and young-child care and early socialization, but the fathers take great interest in the welfare of their children and spend a lot of time playing with them — especially when they are very young. "!Kung fathers — indulgent, affectionate, and devoted — also form very intense mutual attachments with their children. . . . Fathers, like mothers, are not viewed as figures of awesome authority, and their relationships with their children are intimate, nurturant, and physically close" (Shostak 1981, 45).

In all foraging societies the bonds between children of both sexes and their fathers are strong. Nevertheless, at a certain age — different in different societies — young girls begin to spend less time with their fathers than they do with their mothers, and conversely, young boys begin to spend more time with their fathers.

> Until his young son or daughter reached the age of five or six, the behavior of a father was identical toward them. When a newborn infant was in the mother's *amautaq* [carrying sling] the father played fondly with it, holding its arms and caressing its cheeks while gently talking and teasing the infant with the hope of provoking a smile. Sometimes the father would hold the baby himself. After the age of three or four body contact gradually diminished, while the playful relationship involving slight teasing continued. The father made some of the toys his children played with, such as ice toys or spinning toys of bone.
>
> After the age of four or five the father-son relationship grew more intense. The boy watched his father at work, patiently and silently, observing each gesture. (Balikci 1970, 104–5)

The band is made up of several of these smaller family units that camp, gather, and hunt together. But the entire band — and many individuals in other bands — are "family" too. Almost all social relationships in foraging societies are founded upon blood or marriage ties, and where these ties do not exist, kinlike ties are created. Thus a fundamental characteristic of the environment for learning in gathering-and-hunting societies is that children are always among their relations, and it is interesting to note that most foraging groups call themselves simply "The People."

This closeness, this deep current of relationship and connection with virtually every person in the world of the society (and the physical proximity to them on a day-to-day basis), describes an interdependence that, again, is difficult for people in a large industrial society to grasp. Kin relations, closeness, and the security they bring are fundamental to learning in gathering-and-hunting societies, but it is important to see this context of closeness not so much as a rigid dimension of social control (as it is often conceived to be by Westerners) but as an all-pervading dimension that, like the relationship gathering-and-hunting peoples have with the physical environment, provides a framework for social life. Among the Mardudjara aborigines of the Western Australia desert, for example, kinship

> gives people a strong sense of security and well being that stems from their envelopment within a universe of kin, with all of whom some feeling of mutual obligation and responsibility ideally exists. . . . I have never heard Mardudjara express resentment or frustration at the restrictions that their kinship system places on them. Instead, people talk with satisfaction about the good feelings that come from being surrounded by so many others who are "one family" and "one people" with them. (Tonkinson 1978, 45)

And according to Lorna Marshall,

> The !Kung are dependent for their living on belonging to a band. They must belong; they can live no other way. They are also extremely dependent emotionally on the sense of belonging and companionship. Separation and loneliness are unendurable to them. I believe their wanting to belong and be near is actually visible in the way families cluster together in an encampment and in the way they sit huddled together, often touching someone, shoulder against shoulder, ankle across ankle. Security and comfort for them lie in their belonging to their group, free from the threat of rejection and hostility. (1976, 350)

In the sense that all the individuals in the group are related through either blood or marriage, all the adults in the group are, to some extent, mothers and fathers, grandmothers and grandfathers, brothers and sisters. An Mbuti child, for example "knows his real mother and father, of course, and has a special affection for them and they for him, but from an early age he learns that he is the child of [all the adults in the group], for they are all children of the forest" (Turnbull 1961, 128).

CHILDREN AND THE CONTEXT OF CLOSENESS

One of the more striking similarities among gathering-and-hunting societies is that they are all "child centered" (Tonkinson 1978). In every foraging society the children provide "the emotional focus of the household" (Helm 1961) but are often expected to provide little or nothing in the way of foodgetting or help for adults until well into adolescence. Among the !Kung, the Australian aborigines, the Mbuti, the Malaya Semang, and others, males are not expected to begin hunting on a regular basis until they are married and have begun their own families. Adolescent males may hunt and contribute to the welfare of the group, but they are not *expected* to do so by the adult members of the band. Females in these societies begin their productive lives earlier, inasmuch as they are generally quite a bit younger than males at marriage. In all gathering-and-hunting societies the adults are described by ethnographers as indulgent with children. Children always "get their way."

As with all other characteristics of the foraging way of life, the central position of children is inextricably connected with the closeness of all the people in the society to one another and to the external environment. In an evolutionary sense, the children born to an extended family represent that family's wealth. Although the children do not usually become responsible for foodgetting in the society until well after they have the physical capacity to do so, they are of central importance in the band and serve to unite other members of the group. Among the !Kung, for example, there are few divorces after the first child is born (Shostak 1981). Similarly, Briggs notes the importance of a little girl in an Utku Eskimo family: "Indeed, in some respects Saarak was more important than her father. She was the lodestone not only of her household but of her whole kin group" (1970, 107–8).

Since the children are always in close proximity to the adults, they actually help *determine* adult roles and reality. June Helm saw that the children in the Athapaskan group she studied were "agents of social control" because they were "*par excellence*, seekers and disseminators of information in general and of titillating gossip in particular, and the possibility of being gossiped about is, for a Slavey, often an effective inhibitory sanction" (1961, 112).

Because children are generally unrestrained and rarely coerced or disciplined, they are free to spread gossip about and make fun of adults without regard for possible consequences. Adults are almost always under the children's eyes, cognizant that they are being observed. They see their behavior replicated in children's play. They know that almost everything they do will be known and commented upon by the children sooner or later.

Children in foraging societies are thus not only brought up in a social environment that is characterized by intense family and kinship ties, they *contribute*, by their very presence, to that closeness, to the identity of individual adults in the group, and to the group's very understanding of what it means to be an adult. They are not superfluous to adult social relations but significant and active social operators. Husbands and wives are bound more closely through their children, and entire kin groups may be more closely united in their interest in and concern for the children that are born to them. What a powerful impetus this feeling of worth and significance must be to the learning of the young in these societies! Imagine the confidence to try new things and to explore and challenge the environment that develops in such children.

The reciprocal obligations that derive from the sexual division of labor in gathering-and-hunting societies are vital to the survival of not only the core family but the group as a whole. In all of these societies the balances between the efforts of males and females are crucial, but these balances are rarely one-to-one. For example, in all but the foraging societies of the far north, where plant food is of no consequence, gathered food accounts for between 60 and 80 percent of the average daily diet (Lee and DeVore 1968). The people of these societies, however, seem to be fonder of meat than of vegetable foods. The !Kung speak of being "meat hungry" when the hunting has been bad, no matter what vegetable foods may be available (Shostak 1981.) Meat is shared among the whole group, while plant foods are usually eaten by only the immediate family. The women have the greater responsibility for child care; the men often have greater responsibiltiy for the ceremonial life of the band.

Among the Eskimos and Athapaskan and Algonkian Indians of the Canadian north, where women do not contribute to the food supply through gathering (although they are often engaged in certain aspects of hunting and fishing), other reciprocal balances have developed. Women in Eskimo societies sew all the clothing and cook all the food. In addition they, like women in all gathering-and-hunting societies, have primary responsibility for child care. Men in Eskimo societies hunt and, like the men of many other nomadic foraging societies, have primary responsibility for ceremonial activities.

In the next chapter we will examine the attention structure of foraging societies and explore in some detail the ramifications of the sexual division of labor for the learning of the young, but the point to be made here is that the relations of reciprocity between husband and wife lie at the heart of any foraging band's success in subsistence. Marriage is a relationship of economic interdependence as well as reproductive necessity or social convention. If a couple find that they cannot get along, they usually separate—especially if there are no children. Divorce, particularly in first marriages, is rather common in these societies, and though kin may urge couples to stay together, separations based on irreconcilable differences are not condemned. At the same time, marriages that weather the initial adjustment period usually last a lifetime (Shostak 1981).

CULTURAL TIES THAT BIND

The elaborate cultural conventions that have developed in all foraging societies to bind people to one another further reflect the ancient primate need to belong to the group and be reassured that others are part of the group too. In these societies, culture builds upon and reinforces biology.

All foraging societies have well-defined arrangements that govern the division of meat after a successful hunt. As noted above, these distribution conventions are usually related to kin connections, but there are also, as in the case of the Eskimo, meat-sharing partnerships that do not follow kin lines (Balikci 1970).

The !Kung hunter's kill belongs to the owner of the arrow that slays the animal, regardless of who shot it. Arrows are given as gifts—women, children, and the aged can own them—and the owner of the arrow divides the meat among others. "There is much giving and lending of arrows. The society seems to want to extinguish in every way possible the concept of the meat belonging to the hunter" (Marshall 1976, 359). In this context it is interesting to note that often the successful hunter receives the least choice portion of meat, and this convention further diffuses the advantages of ownership. No matter what an individual hunter's skill, the vagaries of stalking game, the factors of luck, being in the right place at the right time, and so on, "there is an unstated conviction that everything evens out in the long run" (Tonkinson 1978, 37).

An interesting aspect of the context of closeness and cooperation in nomadic foraging societies is conversation. People seek one another out, keep up on all the latest news, talk before, during, and after the hunt, tell jokes, and tease one another. "The Mardudjara are great storytellers and love to talk about happenings seen and those unseen but heard about through the desert 'grapevine.' . . . Also characteristic are a gregariousness, a love of animated discussion and repartee, and a keen interest in what transpires in all dimensions" (Tonkinson 1978, 127).

From the perspective of a modern society, in which there are so many occasions for novelty, it may seem that people living together in such intimacy would have said all there was to say to one another long ago, but the talk never flags, and the stories are always interesting. Marshall's description of conversation among the !Kung may almost certainly be applied to every other nomadic foraging society.

> [Conversation] keeps up good, open communication among the members of the band; through its constantly flowing expression it is a salutary outlet for emotions, and it serves as the principal sanction in social discipline. . . .
>   . . . The !Kung are the most loquacious people I know. Conver-

sation in a !Kung encampment is a constant sound like the sound
of a brook, and as low and lapping, except for shrieks of laughter.
(1976, 351)

Much of what the children in these societies learn is acquired through
talking and listening to talk. In this way, living harmoniously in such
close proximity to one another remains possible. The lines of communication are always open, and the openness of access permits intense closeness. Conversation not only ties people together and allows them to work
through the ups and downs of social life, but it also helps define for the
young what sociality is.

People in nomadic foraging societies are further tied together by the
ceremonies that have evolved to mark the important thresholds of life,
common perceptions of the spirit world, and the explanations for the
unknown they all share. The way shamans among the Netsilik Eskimo
heal members of the band is very different from the healing practice of
the *mabarn* of the Mardudjara in Australia, and the healing ceremonies
of these two societies are nothing like the *!kia* of the !Kung. But all these
activities are directed toward healing or making members of the group
whole, and perhaps less obviously, all draw power from the common
conviction of all the people that they are efficacious. Everyone acknowledges the forces that make the healing possible.*

!Kia and its setting of the !Kia dance, serves many functions. It is
the !Kung's primary expression of a religious existence and a cos-
mological perspective. It provides healing and protection, being a
magico-medical mode of coping with illnesses and misfortune. The
!Kia at the dance also increases social cohesion and solidarity. It
allows the individual and communal release of hostility. (Katz
1976, 286)

The lines of connection and closeness to the external environment and
to fellow band members intersect in networks that ensure the survival of

* The intense closeness, the shared assumptions, and the commonly understood patterns
of the external environment and of social life may be better understood when one listens
to a recording of a !Kung healing dance or views one of the outstanding films made by the
Marshalls.

all as long as food is to be had and any are able to get it. These networks also guarantee the opportunity for full participation of every member in the life of the group. The small size of these societies makes it relatively easy to keep track of these connections, and the absolute meaning these connections have for every individual in the group ensures their perpetuation.

Children are full participants in the life of the band. They have great significance in the group and consequently easily acquire a high level of self-esteem (Shostak 1981; Turnbull 1961; see also chapter 6). This "ego strength" and the security that comes with the knowledge that everyone in the band is related to them, cares for them, and will look out for them allows these children to be very active learners indeed. They take risks in their explorations, engage in joking imitations of adults with little fear of reprisal, and observe the full range of adult activity in the camp. In addition, the lessons of cooperation, sharing, and reciprocity come naturally to children in a band because these interactions are more than social ideals. They are ever-present in daily life and are crucial to the survival of the group.

INDIVIDUAL IDENTITY AND STATUS

The emphasis on closeness and unity in the section above may give the impression that people in hunting-and-gathering societies are always in some sort of Rousseauean harmony, always concerned for one another, and always connected. What Marshall says of the !Kung, however, may be generalized to describe other foraging bands: "Their security and comfort must be achieved side-by-side with self-interest and much jealous watchfulness" (1976, 350). Life in nomadic foraging societies has in common with life in other primate societies a dynamic balance between the ties that bind and the need of all to establish identity and status in the group and to look out for themselves. Children in these societies thus learn not only how to cooperate and share and how the rules of reciprocity are observed but also how to assert their individual will and identity and win acknowledgment and status from the other members of the group.

One might say that individuality is guaranteed in a foraging society. The size of the group that forms the band is small enough to admit no strangers; everyone knows so much about everyone else. One could not escape this individuality if one wanted to, and it creates another major part of the backdrop against which all activities of life and learning in these societies take place. Consider Turnbull's description of an Mbuti family:

> [Ekianga] was a very great hunter. . . . He was hairy, broad-chested, and powerful almost to the point of ugliness. . . . He always built his huts in a different shape from everyone else's and in the Pygmy camp near the village his house was the biggest and the smartest of them all, sheltering his entire menage. His youngest wife was a beautiful girl called Kamikan. She was even lighter than most Pygmies, yellowish-brown instead of the more usual coffee-brown. Her brother and mother also lived with the same hunting group. [Her brother] Amabosu was a very temperamental Pygmy. He was a fine hunter, but he was particularly renowned as the best singer and best drummer and best dancer in the area; for these qualities alone his prestige was enormous. His skinny old mother, Sau, was not without fame of her own. Old and infirm people, amongst the Pygmies, are regarded, not exactly with suspicion or mistrust, but with apprehension. (1961, 35)

Turnbull suggests that status in a gathering-and-hunting band is directly related both to the level of one's skill in particular areas and to personal qualities. Both expertise and eccentricity are obvious to all, demonstrated in the context of skills all share and activities all engage in. Ekianga was "a very great hunter," and Amabosu was "the best singer and best drummer and best dancer in the area."

At first these distinctions suggest a paradox, for there is little specialization of function in hunter-gatherer societies. Everyone hunts, sings, drums, and dances. All are engaged in the same activities, more or less, though not necessarily at the same time or in the same sequence. But it is in precisely this context of skill that all share and acknowledge as essential to survival, that status is gained, leadership developed, and power exercised.

Conventions of reciprocity prevent the institutionalization of power and leadership. But if a hunter continually returns with large game, everyone witnesses his success—his perfection of the skills all other men exercise—in spite of any arrangements either by him or the society to diffuse his singularity. Each individual in a band is perfectly aware of what it takes to excel in a particular activity. Everyone is using the same criteria for judgment of performance, so to speak.

In large societies, however, celebrity is often simply a matter of public exposure, and the criteria for judging performance are muddled. While all the members of a hunting-and-gathering band are engaged in the determination of their individual identity and place within the group, all are making their interpersonal assessments on the basis of criteria that are shared. There is no room for faking it in such a society; the closeness and small size of the group do not allow it.

Specialization of activity in nomadic foraging societies is found largely in the realm of the ceremonial, the medicinal, or the supernatural. Most gathering-and-hunting societies recognize shamans, healers, or ritual leaders, and in most societies it is also acknowledged that not everyone can become such a specialist. Among the !Kung a healing dance occurs anywhere from once or twice a week to several times a week, and although all are involved in the ceremony, either dancing or singing, only certain people actually go into the healing trance, or receive *n/um,* as the !Kung say. The ability to receive n/um and use it effectively for healing is respected by the society as an important achievement. Individuals take pride in being n/um masters (Katz 1976, 1982). A Netsilik shaman, or *angatkok,* is "generally respected and feared for his supernatural powers," according to Balikci (1970, 225), and among the Mardudjara of Australia, "men who most often use their special powers for socially approved ends are termed Mabarn throughout the Western Desert" (Tonkinson 1978, 107).

One would think it inevitable that, given the importance of healing and ceremony in nomadic foraging societies, practitioners in these areas would have a kind of generalized status in the group and would become official leaders. But leadership, influence, and status are very complex in societies that exist in a direct relationship with the physical environment and are as small and close as these groups are.

Nothing in their appearance or demeanor distinguishes Mabarn from their fellows, and as specialists they practice part-time only, since all their other activities are the same as those of other men. Their distinctiveness lies in their possession of special skill, knowledge, and psychic powers that give them greater and more effective access to the spiritual realm. (Tonkinson 1978, 107)

In daily life the Netsilik shaman "behaved like an ordinary hunter" (Balikci 1970, 225), and a !Kung n/um master "remains an ordinary person during his non !Kia state rather than an intimate of the gods or a chosen instrument" (Katz 1976, 294).

There are rarely official positions in gathering-and-hunting societies (though there is certainly leadership), little generalization of authority from one activity to another, and no social hierarchy that exists outside of personal merit and relationships such as kinship described above. Decisions are made and status is achieved in this seemingly unlikely context, but the process is hard for Westerners to understand for it includes everything about the people's present way of life, the past, and the spirit world. The process of acquiring status and influence has no beginning or end, and as Hart and Pilling say of the Tiwi in Northern Australia, "any attempt to describe the operations involved . . . must perforce start in the middle" (1979, 52).

Another important aspect of status, influence, and leadership in foraging societies is that they are more like an acceptance of responsibility than an assumption of authority—more like moderating a discussion than telling others what to do:

Perhaps the most crucial aspect of the balance of power [in !Kung society] is the process of leadership and decision making. Determining how the !Kung actually make important decisions is quite difficult. With no formal leaders or hierarchies, and no political or legal institutions to convey authority, decisions are made on the basis of group consensus. Each group has individuals whose opinions carry more weight than those of others—because of age, of having ancestors who have lived in the area longer, or of personal attributes such as intelligence, knowledge or charisma. These people tend to be more prominent in group discussion, to make their opinions known and their suggestions clear, and to articulate the consensus once it is determined. Despite their lack of formal authority, they function very much as group leaders. (Shostak 1981, 245)

Turnbull says that "Pygmies dislike and avoid personal authority, though they are by no means devoid of a sense of responsibility. It is rather that they think of responsibility as communal" (1961, 125).

As in all human societies (and, for that matter, in the primate societies described in part 1), every member of a gathering-and-hunting society is concerned with his or her personal, individual identity and status in the group. But the status one may achieve in these societies is not in-stitutionalized; no one can mistake a position of authority for personal identity. Those who achieve prominence are those who do things best and facilitate clarity and consensus in the group. Because every skill and area of knowledge is important for survival and well-being in these societies, status, power, and influence are remarkably diffused through-out the members: between men and men, women and women, men and women, parents and children, and young and old.

The children of foraging societies learn about and acquire individual identity and status in an environment that supports and encourages such acquisitions yet also supports and encourages cooperative, collective behavior. Thus children discover not only how to view themselves as unique individuals but how that individuality is connected to the needs of the group and the rewards of communal life. The balances between the need to belong and the need to achieve individual status ensure that everyone in a gathering-and-hunting band can be competent, because the skills that all share are of ultimate importance. Nearly everyone can excel in one area or another. The lines of individual identity and status in gathering-and-hunting societies, like the lines of relationship and recip-rocal obligation, crisscross and overlap. Like food, status is available to everyone. Everyone knows what competence consists of, so it does not have to be demonstrated through competition. Hunters do not need to vie with one another; gatherers need not struggle to bring in the biggest load. There are so many ways in which to distinguish oneself—ways that are recognized by and important to all the other members of the group—that everyone is distinguished.

This setting is the socioemotional environment in which human chil-dren have grown and learned for most of the species' existence. And the extraordinarily complex relationships between what individuals need and what the group needs have formed a good part of the *content* of children's learning for all this time. A look at the specific relationships that make up the attention structure of hunting-and-gathering societies should help clarify the process through which this social learning is done.

6

The Social Context of Learning
in Foraging Societies

THE emotional systems described in chapter 5 impel children to learn specific *essentials* of social life. They need to discover how to subsist in the natural environment, what it means to be a man or a woman, what it means to be an adult in general, and what the needs of younger children are so that they can become competent parents themselves.

MEN AND WOMEN: GENDER IDENTITY AND ROLES

As children grow and develop they are confronted with clear examples of what it means to be a man or a woman. The primary constituent of their individual identities is the awareness that they are male or female and, perhaps more important, that it is *good* to be a girl becoming a woman or a boy becoming a man. The connection to the physical environment for survival ensures that these identities will include knowledge about cooperating, compromising, reciprocating, and attending to others; and the essential equality of the male and female dimensions of experience ensures that a child will not have to assume a gender role at the expense of personal identity.

The sexual division of labor in nomadic foraging societies is an intricately balanced system of expectation, duty, understanding, and emotional bond. This system and the other reciprocal relations that flow from it are crucial elements of a child's learning in these societies, where gender identity is a paramount constituent of personal identity.

Perhaps the most important aspect of male-female relations and the division of labor in hunting-and-gathering societies is that the value of the respective gender-specific activities is equivalent. What Lee says of the !Kung can be extended to most if not all foraging groups: "On balance, the evidence shows a relatively equal role in society for the two sexes, and the !Kung data certainly do not support a view of women in 'the state of nature' as oppressed or dominated by men or as subject to sexual exploitation at the hands of males" (1979, 454). Tonkinson (1978) describes gender relations among the Mardudjara aborigines of Western Australia in a similar manner. Jane Goodale writes of the Tiwi of Melville Island in northern Australia: "Although the opportunities for prestige and self-expression do not appear to be as great for the female as for the male Tiwi, the basic equality of the two sexes as unique individual members of the society is stressed in the culture" (1971, 338). "Appear" is the critical word here, and according to Goodale (and Berndt 1981), the appearances can be deceiving. Goodale emphasizes what she calls the "different character of the male-female world." She suggests that, while "personal achievement seems to be the dominant value for which Tiwi males and females strive during their existence in the world of the living" (p. 335), this achievement comes, and is measured, in different ways for males and females.

It is a mistake to compare the authority and status of men and women in these societies in a simplistic or linear fashion. The status of each and the ways of measuring that status exist in two different dimensions — much like the axes of dominance and matrifocality in primate groups described in part 1. Western observers have tended to focus on the lines of "official" status and on the ceremonial and magical areas of life, which are more often the province of men. But the *actual* workings of authority and influence in a gathering-and-hunting band appear to be more intricate and equitable than the official lines indicate (see Goodale 1971; Shostak 1981; Lee 1979; Dahlberg 1981).

Much of the power and status of women is covert in foraging societies because a woman's position is so obvious to the band. Women in these groups are the "life force" (Turnbull 1961), for they bring children into the world. Of course, one must not oversimplify. But it seems that the unquestioned importance of children in gathering-and-hunting societies and the deep ties that accompany mother-child relations form the foundation of one dimension of status, influence, and identity (as it does in all higher primate societies), while the importance of meat and matters ceremonial forms the foundation of another. Shostak quotes one of the few female n/um masters in the Dobe area:

> I am a master at trancing to drum-medicine songs. I lay hands on people and they usually get better. I know how to trick God from wanting to kill someone and how to have God give the person back to me. But I, myself, have never spoken directly to God nor have I seen or gone to where he lives. I am still very small when it comes to healing and I haven't made these trips. . . . I am a woman, and women don't do most of the healing. They fear the pain of the medicine inside them because it really hurts! I don't really know why women don't do more of it. Men just fear it less. It's really funny—women don't fear childbirth, but they fear medicine! (Shostak 1981, 303)

It is also important to see that the specific roles of the sexual division of labor in day-to-day situations are often much more flexible than might be expected. The most powerful healer in the Dobe region during the time Katz studied the healing ceremonies of the !Kung was a woman (Katz 1982). There are strict divisions of labor and activity, but in the larger context of life in a nomadic foraging society, even prohibitions and rigid customs become pieces of a great puzzle of reciprocity and balance. While Netsilik men do not sew hides, the task of scraping them thin is theirs (Balikci 1970).

Many ceremonies in nomadic foraging societies acknowledge and celebrate both the connections and the differences between men and women. Among the Mbuti the two most important ceremonial activities are the *molimo* and the *elima*. The molimo is a kind of multipurpose ceremony used for healing, for what might be called "community building," and in general "the Pygmies call out their *molimo* whenever things seem to be going wrong" (Turnbull 1961, 91). At first Turnbull thought that the molimo was exclusively for men, but then one night, without any preparation that Turnbull could devine, the molimo ceremony was joined by the women of the band and an old woman who was visiting the camp.

> There is an old legend that once it was the woman who "owned" the molimo, but the men stole it from them and ever since the women have been forbidden to see it. Perhaps this [the addition of the women to the ceremony and the resultant "binding" of the men] was a way of reminding the men of the origin of their molimo. There is another old legend which tells that it was a woman who stole fire from the chimpanzees or, in yet another version, from the great forest spirit. I did not understand it by any means, but somehow it seemed to make sense. (Turnbull 1961, 154)

The elima ceremony among the Mbuti is organized and run by the women to mark a girl's first menstrual period. But the young men of the village are important participants in the elima, and a "father of the elima" is designated from among the girl's older kinsmen.

Though there is "men's work" and "women's work" in nomadic foraging societies, this way of life is one in which the dimensions of male and female experience overlap and interact continually. !Kung men, for example, often gather vegetable foods when returning from an unsuccessful hunt, and even more consistently they relay information about the location of plant foods to the women. At the same time, the women report on the animal spoor they have seen while gathering and often take an active and influential part in the prehunt conversation (Lee and DeVore 1976). Mbuti women and children beat the jungle to drive animals into the nets of the waiting men (Turnbull 1961), and Eskimo women and children help in the spring seal hunt and in the construction of salmon weirs. A Netsilik couple builds an igloo cooperatively; the man works inside the structure and the woman works outside (Balikci 1970).

The sexual division of labor in nomadic foraging societies has evolved in such a way that different but complementary and equivalent realms of activity and experience exist for men and women. Associated with these dimensions of experience are subsistence success, family and kinship structures, and spiritual meaning—all, in short, that children in these societies must learn about. In addition, this system has evolved in a way that ensures reciprocity and equality and allows the people to avoid competition between the sexes.

The sense of self-esteem that young people in these societies acquire as they mature sexually is well demonstrated in a story told by Marjorie Shostak.

> One day I noticed a twelve-year-old girl, whose breasts had just started to develop, looking into the small mirror beside the driver's window of our Land Rover. She looked intently at her face, then, on tip-toe, examined her breasts and as much of her body as she could see, then went to her face again. She stepped back to see more, moved in again for a closer look. She was a lovely girl, although not outstanding in any way except by being in the full health and beauty of youth. She saw me watching. I teased in the !Kung manner I had by then thoroughly learned, "So ugly! How is such a young girl already so ugly?" She laughed. I asked, "You don't agree?" She beamed, "No, not at all. I'm beautiful!" She continued to look at herself. I said, "Beautiful? Perhaps my eyes have become broken with age that I can't see where it is?" She said "Everywhere—my face, my body. There's no ugliness at all." These remarks were said easily, with a broad smile, but without arrogance. The pleasure she felt in her changing body was as evident as the absence of conflict about it. (1981, 269–70)

The *inevitability* of the roles of both men and women in hunting-and-gathering societies is an important point. Boys will become hunters, toolmakers, fathers; girls will become gatherers, makers of their own tools, mothers. Living these lives rewards men and women both and gives them opportunities to be part of the larger group and acquire personal status. The inevitability is thus not oppressive. On the contrary, it contributes to individual self-confidence and the general security that facilitates learning.

OVERLAPPING GENERATIONS

In every foraging society three and sometimes four generations are ever-present, and grandparents are important people in the environment of learning (see Mead 1970). Old folks in these societies, freed from the most arduous activities of subsistence, have a great deal of leisure time and often spend it with children (Turnbull 1961; Balikci 1970). Thus a considerable amount of what children learn is acquired through association with the older generation.

From the elders children not only gain general knowledge and skill and the history and lore of the group; they also learn firsthand how it feels to be old. They can see how the elderly struggle to keep up with the nomadic band and hear the complaints of those who are not well provided for by their children or grandchildren. As children are thus presented with direct examples of the responsibilities they will eventually have for their own parents and grandparents, they are simultaneously presented with true images of the aging process.

THE GENERAL ADULT CONTEXT

A child in a nomadic foraging society is constantly exposed to and interacting with adults of many ages and degrees of relationship—adults who are all doing similar tasks within the gathering-and-hunting life-style but who have distinct personalities, areas of expertise, likes and dislikes, and amounts of status in particular circumstances. The importance of the adult context for children cannot be overemphasized, for in observing and imitating (and learning from the mistakes of) adults in the band, children learn the skill, the knowledge, and the responsibilities of adulthood. They refine and check the things imparted to them through the immediate family structure and learn what the boundaries of behavior actually are (as opposed to what they are said to be), what status consists of and how it is achieved, and how problems may be solved.

Adult life is wide open to the young in a foraging band. They know how arguments between adults arise and are resolved (or lead to more drastic ruptures). They see how different adults pursue similar or different ends. All around the children, at all times, adults who all have the same skills are using them in individually different ways and with varying degrees of success. The children see that a great hunter may be a less skillful singer. In all foraging societies the children experience, first through observation and then through direct involvement, the confusion, the intensity, the danger, and the pleasure of sexuality, for "nothing is hidden in the igloo" (Balikci 1970) or in a hut that is part of an encampment of ten or fifteen similar huts.

Without institutionalized positions to flatten out personalities and routinize interpersonal relations, young people perceive adults in foraging societies as complex, changeable beings who have both success and failure, who are at times joyful and at other times downcast, who argue and love and sing and dance. Children are close by way of kinship, marriage, or simply intense daily association with *every* adult member of the band and thus have a range of role models with which they might identify or from which they might appropriate bits of skill, knowledge, and behavior in the formation of their own identities.

OTHER CHILDREN

Just as children in foraging societies learn about what it is to be old by living with and observing the old, just as they learn about adulthood by watching and interacting with different adults, they learn about children (and themselves) from being in close contact with other children constantly.

> At Apa Lelo, [the children's *bopi*, or playground] was on the shore
> where the river twisted around an island and one branch of it cut
> in almost between Cephu's camp and the main camp. The water
> was fairly shallow there, and all day long the children splashed and
> wallowed about to their heart's content. If they tired of that, they
> had a couple of vine swings in their *bopi*; one was a small one for
> younger children, and the other was hung from two tall trees.
> Infants watched with envy as the older children swung wildly about,
> climbing high up on the vine strands and performing all sorts of
> acrobatics. (Turnbull 1961, 128)

Children are not segregated by age in gathering-and-hunting societies. If the group is large enough and there are a number of children who are roughly the same age, age-mate play groups form (Balikci 1970; Helm 1961), but these groups are by no means exclusive, nor are they institutionalized in any way by the adults. The children form their own relationships. Among the !Kung "a typical band of children pointed temporarily in some play in the village might include a 5-year-old boy, an 11-year-old girl, a 14-year-old boy, and a 1-year-old toddler hanging on the fringe of the action" (Draper 1976, 202). Among the Lynx Point Athapaskans "we find the self-conscious, seventeen-year-old Eddie playing tag with a four-year-old" (Helm 1961, 94).

Older children provide models for younger children, and of course, older children learn about babies and toddlers by observing their younger brothers and sisters and those of other families. It should be emphasized that the older children are never forced or trained to assume responsibility for their younger siblings. This responsibility may indeed be assumed, for older children inevitably become the leaders of the play group and thus automatically accept a certain responsibility for the younger children. In this way they learn about responsibility. But these older children are not held *accountable* by the adults for the safety, the instruction, or the behavior of the younger children.

NATURAL DISCIPLINE: COMPELLING ATTENTION

The discipline of the young, as we understand it in modern technological society, is a mode of compelling attention so that children may learn what we want them to know and may behave in an acceptable manner. Little of what we would consider discipline occurs in nomadic foraging societies. As noted in chapter 5, the behavior of children in these societies is rarely constrained. Children are almost never beaten and have leeway to do pretty much as they please.

In many gathering-and-hunting societies maturation is described as the acquisition of something. The Utku Eskimo say that a child acquires *ihuma*, which "refers to all functions that we think of as cerebral: mind, thought, memory, reason, sense, ideas, will" (Briggs 1970, 375). The !Kung explain the tantrums and disobedience of young children by saying that their intelligence has not yet come to them.

> There is no doubt in the parents' mind that as children grow up they will learn to act with sense, with or without deliberate training, simply as a result of maturation, social pressure and the desire to

conform to group values. Since most !Kung adults are cooperative, generous, and hard-working, and seem to be no more self-centered than any other people, this theory is evidently right, at least for them. (Shostak 1981, 149)

Parents and other adults in gathering-and-hunting societies are likely as indulgent and patient as they are because the only option for a child in a foraging society is to become an adult in a foraging society: "What else is there for [Mbuti children] to learn except to grow into good adults?" (Turnbull 1961, 128).

Adulthood in these societies has the same inevitable quality about it as sexual identity, for although there is considerable opportunity for individual expression in such a society, the *framework* of life is not a matter of choice—integrated as it is with the cycles of the physical environment, and balanced as it is between individual and collective needs. Thus many of the occasions for discipline that confront parents in a large modern society simply never come up in foraging societies. Children need not be forced to comply with their parents' wishes, because at an early age they begin imitating (and assessing) their parents' behavior and activity and gradually become contributing members of the band themselves. There is no need to make children do things "for their own good," because there is no difference between what is good for them and what is good for everybody else, or no difference between what they see going on all around them and what their adult lives will consist of. The discipline-like activities we do see occasionally in gathering-and-hunting societies are most often a reflection of lost patience or momentary anger on the part of an adult, rather than demands for generalized obedience or ideological compliance.

By far the most common form of discipline of young children in all foraging societies is joking and ridicule. Children are teased and scolded humorously. If they get angry at the teasing, they are not punished for demonstrating their anger. More important, this disciplinary strategy is not reserved for children but is a common mode of interaction among *all* the members of the band, regardless of age.

THE SOCIAL CONTEXT OF HUMAN LEARNING:
A BRIEF SUMMARY

For thousands of years human children have grown to maturity in small bands made up of families bound together by kinship and other reciprocal ties. In such groups children have acquired personal identity and individual status within a context of common activity. In all those years the sexual division of labor and different dimensions of experience for males and females characterized the social environment in which children discovered their personal identities and ensured the equality of the participants in the male-female partnership. No matter what environment the band lived in, no matter what its cultural idiosyncrasies, children have, until rather recently, grown up witnessing adult behavior in a wide range of situations, seeing the elderly change and die, and seeing babies arrive and grow.

These realities of the human social environment call forth the biologically based emotions associated with belonging and individual importance, reciprocity, childcare, and so forth. These emotions in turn form the basis for the social behavior the child must learn. In this social environment the active human organism makes its investigations and discoveries.

It should be clear at this point that any learning system for children should provide for a smooth transition from childhood to adulthood. The framework for a child's discovery of the rules and opportunities of social life should be formed by a balance between the need to belong and the need to acquire status. Social roles and realities should be presented to children clearly. Everything that children learn should contribute to their survival in the physical environment and to their becoming competent members of their group.

7

How Children in Foraging Societies Learn

IN CHAPTER 3 the activities of learning in all higher primate societies were identified as observation, imitation, play, and investigative behavior, or exploration. These same activities occupy the bulk of a young child's time in every gathering-and-hunting band. They form a complex of daily activity that is beautifully matched to the kinds of knowledge and skill children must acquire for success and well-being in life.

From the carrying sling, infants watch the comings and goings of children and adults alike, observe toolmaking, storytelling, dancing, singing, and fighting. Little is done out of their sight, for they go everywhere with their mothers.

As children grow older and begin to spend more time among peers, they, like all children everywhere, actively imitate others—adults, other children, even animals—and these imitations become games. Children play at what they see going on around them, but even more, they explore, through activities that are obviously pleasurable, the range of the social and physical environments. Two examples from different hunting-and-gathering groups should suffice to establish this point.

The [Malaya Semang] children were sitting contentedly, and very silent, apart in the forest, hidden by the undergrowth. "What are you doing there?" I asked little Bunga.

"Making *hanya* [huts]," he answered, meaning that they were playing house.

They had made little shelters [hanya] in exact imitation of the big ones, and sleeping-places of bamboo. There they were sitting in families, man and wife, all with lighted cigars in their mouths. The fire was burning on the hearth and they were going to do the cooking. They had all decked themselves with flowers and foliage. (Schebesta 1927, 82)

As her hunting skills increase the *kitjina* [Tiwi girl] begins to join other children of both sexes in independent expeditions. The children wander about the bush in a gang, playing tag and singing as they go. The boys may take potshots at birds, throwing stones high into the trees and making a contest of it. The girls collect berries, small fruits, and bird's eggs. If anything worthy of cooking is found and they are far from camp, the gang will make a fire, cook, and carefully portion out the food. I once saw one rather small fish divided among eight hungry children. (Goodale 1971, 38)

Through exactly such activities the young of all higher primates acquire skill and knowledge. Though the play of human children and chimpanzee young may be worlds apart in content and complexity, the activity is unquestionably play for both species. It is structured by the young themselves, contains elements of adult behavior, and is intensely pleasurable and exciting.

Two other characteristics of children's learning in foraging societies bear striking resemblance to learning in other primate societies: (1) there is virtually no formal instruction by adults or older children associated with children's observation, imitation, play, or exploration; and (2) with an important exception (see "Formal Instruction in Foraging Societies" below), these are the same activities through which adults continue to learn throughout their lives.

LEARNING BY DOING

In acquiring skill and knowledge related to the activities of daily living — hunting, gathering, and all the complex social relationships that occur in bands—children encounter no attempts by adults to structure their attention formally. Children's observation is rarely directed by adult band members, and if at times the older generation will join in children's games, they do so on the children's terms. Adults never say to children, "Why don't you all go play *hanya*," much less show children *how* to play. Indeed, it appears that there is a conscious acknowledgment of the value and necessity of learning from experience in nomadic foraging societies. Consider the following brief examples.

Goodale writes of the Tiwi:

> We have seen that very young children are allowed literally to play with fire, and never once did I hear a parent telling their child, "Now be careful, dear." The maxim "experience is the best teacher" seems to be rigidly followed. . . . Generally parents or other adults will only interfere in their child's activities when they become really dangerous to some other younger child who cannot fend for itself. (1971, 36)

Draper describes a scene in a !Kung encampment:

> One afternoon I watched for 2 hours while a father hammered and shaped the metal for several arrow points. During the period his son and his grandson (both under 4 years old) jostled him, sat on his legs, and attempted to pull the arrow heads from under the hammer. When the boys' fingers came close to the point of impact, he merely waited until the small hands were a little farther away before he resumed hammering. Although the man remonstrated with the boys (about once every 3 minutes), he did not become cross or chase the boys off; and they did not heed his warnings to quit interfering. Eventually, perhaps 50 minutes later, the boys moved off a few steps to join some teenagers lying in the shade. . . .
>
> I never observed a man who was working at this job [dressing antelope hides] attempt to get help from his own or another child. Nor did the man volunteer information or advice about how the job was done. He simply worked with the children squatting at the edge of the hide watching and nibbling with apparent absorption, then moving on to some other pastime. (1976, 206, 212)

Blurton Jones and Konner (1976) provide a clear example of the relationship that exists between the learners and those who know in gathering-and-hunting societies:

> This indirect adult communication of important information seems comparable to the indirect way young men acquire information about animals and technology, which appears to be quite simply a matter of watching and listening to other people and then trying for one's self. There is almost no direct teaching. Indeed, Konner witnessed an enlightening argument between some younger men who hunt very little and some older and more active men. The inactive young men accused the older men of having neglected to teach them hunting. The older men countered that this was not something that one taught anybody, it is something that one just did. "You teach yourself"—a very common phrase among the !Kung—would be applicable here. (1976, 338–39).

Children are rarely, if ever, exhorted to behave one way or another, and lectures, like disciplinary activities, are often the result of situational anger on the part of the adult rather than a mode for the inculcation of "right" attitudes and behaviors. Intelligence will come to all in time.

As with all higher primate societies, there is little separation between the form and content of children's learning in foraging societies. Most of the daily activities are, simply, things one does. You teach yourself; how should these things be learned except by doing them? By playing with fire or knives and by exploring their properties, children learn respect for them soon enough; by playing at sex (see Shostak 1981; Tonkinson 1978), a child learns its power and complexity. Everything must be investigated; experiments must be made. And through these activities a child in a foraging society will grow up to be an adult in a foraging society.

THE ACTIVITIES OF LIFELONG LEARNING

Observation, imitation, play, and exploration do not end with adulthood in hunting-and-gathering bands, and in the main the activities of adult learning are exactly the same as the activities of children's learning. In the course of their investigations into the !Kung knowledge of animal behavior, Blurton Jones and Konner discovered that observation is a critical learning mode throughout adulthood.

> We have evidence that [the !Kung] sometimes observe animals more than is necessary for the purpose of the hunt in which they are involved. For example, one man described courtship of a pair of gemsbok in great detail adding that he was so involved in watching them that he forgot about shooting them, and they went out of sight before he was able to. (1976, 337–38)

In all foraging societies playfulness continues throughout life, and humor, joking, miming, and imitating are important aspects of adult interaction as well as children's play. Husbands and wives joke with each other and with their children. Play is a way of reaffirming, checking, or modifying the social balances that are central to the success of this way of life (Briggs 1979). The activities of children's learning are thus replicated in the adult world and provide all the members of the band with a kind of continuing education.

If there is little or no formal instruction in the learning of day-to-day subsistence techniques, social activities, and fundamental values, one might expect that the transmission of the kinship structure—often extremely complicated and tied to social conventions and ceremonial functions—would involve some teaching. But this appears not to be the case:

> The Mardudjara, realistically, do not expect children, especially small ones, to conform to the kinship system. Children's lives in the desert are remarkably free from restraints and very little pressure is put on them in their socialization. But they are born into a world of kinship statuses; they hear kin terms in constant use; and as soon as they are considered capable of assimilating knowledge, they are taught the should and should-nots of behavior towards various kin. They see the system in action and thus learn both the ideal and actual patterning of social relationships as part of growing up. They absorb the system effortlessly, learning the primacy of of kin cate-

gory as a behavioral guide. . . . Having learned the system, children begin conforming to it in early adolescence without any specific directives from their elders. (Tonkinson 1978, 45)

As with the learning of day-to-day subsistence activities, kinship relations, and fundamental social values, so with the transmission of the history of The People: there seems to be no formal instruction of the children by the adults. "Just as there is no formal education among them, no formal inculcation of mythology occurs and the telling of myths is not given a special place by the Mardudjara in the framework of ritual life (Tonkinson 1978, 94). The !Kung, apparently, are similarly inclined:

> The !Kung seem to have little interest in teaching the lore of their forefathers to the children. The story-telling groups I observed consisted much more frequently of a small group of old people getting together for some real, grownup enjoyment. The telling of stories among San is no watered-down nursery pastime but the substantial adult pleasure of old cronies over a bawdy or horrific or ridiculous tale. Children are not *barred* from listening to the stories, and they do wander in and out of a group of storytelling adults as freely as they do at a trance dance. They may listen with considerable interest for a while. (Biesele 1976, 307)

It is important to note that the adults in these societies are not at all anxious about the way in which children replicate subsistence skills, comprehend the kinship system, preserve social values, or perceive the history of the band. Because all these skills and all this information will come to children as a natural consequence of their membership in the group, the adults need not worry about how learning will take place and whether the child will do it well.

FORMAL INSTRUCTION IN FORAGING SOCIETIES

There is very little formal instruction in foraging societies. When it does take place it is always associated with areas of experience that require unusual abilities and are connected with healing, spiritual consciousness, and the supernatural.*

The amount of teaching varies significantly from culture to culture. Among the Mardudjara, the Mbuti, and the !Kung, even the secrets of healing and the supernatural are transmitted without formal instruction. The shamans, or *mabarn*, of the Mardudjara are "not required to go through the elaborate special initiations modeled on death and rebirth, that have been reported for the Eastern Desert regions" (Tonkinson 1978, 197). The !Kung have many trance-dance healers, both male and female, and although there is support for those who would acquire n/um, there appears to be no special instruction in either its acquisition or its use. "Teaching is primarily by example. The teacher has been there before" (Katz 1976, 295).

On the other hand, among the Eskimo the boys who are to become shamans are selected by the shamans themselves.

> The *angatkoks* [shamans] were in the habit of observing the behavior of boys, to discover if some bright young man had received the call. Once selection had been made, the formal training started. Initially the novice joined the household of an elderly *angatkok*-teacher, where he observed a series of special taboos, such as abstaining from eating outdoors, from eating liver, head, heart or intestines, and from having sexual relations. The novice, assisted by a spirit, slept intermittently and began having visions. Then he moved to a separate igloo where, during a period of several weeks, he was taught the secret vocabulary together with necessary shamanistic techniques and obtained his paraphernalia (a headdress and a belt) from his parents. (Balikci 1970, 225)

Many observers (see, e.g., Strehlow 1970; Meggitt 1962; Maddock 1972) testify to the elaborate formality of the Australian male-initiation rites in some aboriginal bands and to the direct teaching of initiates that

---

*There is surely an important connection between cultural anxiety and the activity of teaching. When these small societies are overpowered by large societies, the attitude of adults toward preservation and accuracy changes, and attempts are made to teach the younger generation the traditional ways.

forms an important component of these ceremonies. A young Northern Aranda man described part of his initiation as follows:

> The old men took me apart from the other young men of my own age at an early date. They showed me many *gura* ceremonies which they withheld from the other members of the bandicoot clan because they were still too young.
>
> My elders kept on repeating these ceremonies time and again in my presence; they were afraid that I might forget them. (Strehlow 1970, 115)

This information came to Strehlow at a time when the Aranda way of life was threatened with extinction, so it is difficult to tell whether the elders' anxiety arose from the kind of information that was being imparted to the young in these ceremonies or whether it was a more generalized anxiety, a fear of losing everything if the young did not carry the culture into succeeding generations.

At the same time, it is important to see that the formal instruction that does occur is an extension of the learning associated with subsistence activities and social dynamics. The activities of the shaman or the healer serve to extend social bonds into other worlds and different states of consciousness. They give people a sense of continuity with their ancestors and with one another, and at the same time they offer individuals the opportunity for profound personal experience, status, and identity.

One might also note that most of the initial learning about ceremony and spiritual matters is derived through observation and listening and by imitating what is seen. From the earliest age, all children know the reasons and meanings of ceremonies, even if they have not been permitted to witness them or do not fully understand them. Among the Walbiri in Australia, "although the youngsters do not attend totemic ceremonies, they often sit with their fathers when the latter discuss ritual matters in all-male company; it is thought that the boys are too young to understand these conversations" (Meggitt 1962, 116).

Noting the way in which young !Kung learn about the acquisition of n/um and the !kia state, Katz writes:

> One of the most striking things about !Kung education for !kia is

that it is very much a normal process of socialization. Every male tries to become a master of n/um, though he may try more or less hard. Many years before a person seriously tries to become a n/um master he is playing with !kia. A group of five- and six-year-olds may perform a small !kia dance, imitating the structure of the dance, the dance steps, and the !kia gestures, at times falling as if in !kia. Through play, the child is modeling; as he grows up, he is learning about !kia. (1976, 289)

Young Mbuti girls hear about the elima from pubescent girls who are either anticipating the ceremony or have just gone through it, and they witness the assault of the initiates on young men at the end of the elima (Turnbull 1961). All children in a foraging band have seen a shaman or healer at work before they are very old. They may not understand the significance or the origin of the words used or the gestures made, but they witness the activities and their results. Certainly if children get sick, they become participants in healing ceremonies.

It is important to see that formal instruction of some kind is not completely foreign to these societies. We do not know how much teaching (if any) took place in early human societies, but it is probably safe to say that formal instruction has been part of human social life for some time. Nevertheless, there are two vital points to be made about formal instruction in foraging societies and the relationship this teaching bears to education in modern industrial societies. First, modern schools have completely reversed the relationship between formal and informal instruction. Our society believes that *all* skills, attitudes, and areas of knowledge must be taught to children formally, while in a hunting-and-gathering band, teaching is reserved for only the most intense or the most rarified personal experiences. Second, the areas of learning that are taught formally in the schools are often unconnected with other aspects of a child's life and thus have no intrinsic meaning. I discuss in part 3 the problems associated with these and other changes in the learning environment.

Part 3
Learning in Contemporary Society

8

The Changed Environment

THE physical environments of large urban societies are nothing like those in which nomadic foraging societies existed for perhaps one million years. The social context of learning is likewise different from the social environments that produced the human learning adaptation. In modern industrial societies divisions between what and how children learn and what they will become are the rule.

When confronted with the tremendous gulf that separates life in, say, a !Kung band from life in New York City, many doubt the usefulness of an evolutionary perspective as a framework for understanding modern societies: "All this about the hunter-gatherers is fine, but so what? Life is very different now." This is true. Humans have, among other things, changed the physical environment radically in much of the world and have upset ecological balances fine-tuned by the processes of evolution for eons. We live in societies of hundreds of millions, maintain contact with every corner of the earth through technological systems, and preserve the information we generate in print, on tape, disk, or film.

The human species is indeed extraordinarily adaptable. We can survive in slums and ghettos, in suburban isolation, or in impersonal organizations, separated from our families. This ability to adapt to new or rapidly changing social and physical environments is sometimes offered as evidence that there are no significant biological constraints on human activity or organization. But our ability as a species to develop this astounding array of phenotypical adaptations has also led us into serious social and environmental trouble.

Part 3 is grounded in the premise that much of our distress and many of our problems stem from the difficulty (often the impossibility) of fulfilling biologically based human needs. Another premise of this argument is that the most poignant evidence for the seriousness of our trouble is to be found in the experiences of children.

So much has been written about the distresses of the modern age that I hesitate to bring them up again. Freud and Marx revolutionized human history by identifying the gulf between what life in modern society actually is and what it should be. But the ideal state for thinkers who feel the imbalance of our times is an intellectual construct, and the underlying question of what we are actually separated from (that is, what our nature actually is) often goes begging. This chapter looks at exemplary characteristics of life in a modern industrial society through the prism of band-society balances. Most if not all of the imbalances one sees from such a perspective have been identified by others and will be familiar to the reader. I have tried to focus on characteristics that are commonly acknowledged as problems and dilemmas and, because this chapter is intended to serve as a backdrop to the problem of children's education, have not attempted a review of the literature of trouble and change.

LOSING TOUCH WITH THE PHYSICAL ENVIRONMENT

Agriculture, or more properly the development of sedentary living, wrought great changes in human society. These changes grew more rapid and complex with the development of more and more sophisticated technology. We are only beginning to comprehend how we have changed. Living permanently in the same place allowed for the accumulation of material wealth, and an assured food supply in association with large numbers contributed to specialization.

The emergence of large, permanent societies destroyed the ancient social balances of the foraging way of life. One of the most serious results was the loss of a direct connection with the natural environment. In modern technological societies the relationship between daily activity and the actual requirements of survival are often extraordinarily abstract.

Certainly pushing a cart through a supermarket is "food getting," but the activity is devoid of meaning when compared with gathering and hunting (or agriculture, for that matter). There are echoes of this gap between what we do and why we do it in the satisfaction we derive or do not derive from our work, and there are important implications of this gap for children's learning.

The natural link between individual survival and community has withered. As societies have grown larger and larger and as humans have refined and extended their abilities to produce food and affect the physical environment, it has become possible to be assured of survival and have absolutely no assurance of well-being. At least one of the results of this separation is alienation—from nature, from one's own feelings, and from the means of subsistence. As Karl Marx said (and every worker on an assembly line knows), the meaningless job that provides money, thus ensuring survival, daily undermines well-being and personal identity.

BREAKING THE TIES THAT BIND

As human civilizations have become larger, the social ties that characterized early human societies have become drastically altered. A modern society like the United States is so large and diffuse that it is impossible to know more than a few members of the population at a time. Although kinship still has some importance in modern societies, families are often scattered in different parts of the country—or even throughout the world. The family structure that was the fundamental unit of human society for so long still exists, but in a highly isolated form. The family in any form is breaking down in many societies.

Reciprocal arrangements still characterize human society, but they too have become abstracted and linearized. Human reciprocity in modern technological societies is often mediated by money, legal systems, or bureaucratic arrangements, all of which act to reduce the multidimensional interactions characteristic of foraging societies to impersonal, quantified balances.

With the breakdown of family life and the reduction of the number of opportunities for intimate cooperation and belonging has come an abstraction of social ties in general. The focus of human care, concern, and loyalty has shifted, at least in part, from kin relations to political, institutional, or special-interest entities. Hundreds of communities form in large societies. Some of these may have connections with kindred (extended, for example, to include ethnicity), but most do not. There are Hispanic communities, gay communities, academic communities, religious communities, scientific communities, and so on. But the commonality represented by the designation *community* may or may not be bound by place, may find its connection in a particular abstraction (e.g., a religion), or only, as in the case of the scientific community, through the *processes* of abstraction. A community may or may not have families at its core and may or may not be neighborly. It may be perceived from without or from within, and it is quite possible for an individual in the United States to belong to several, sometimes contradictory, communities at the same time. We need to be community members, but how do we go about it? Who are The People now?

In modern societies children are often liabilities. Children (and, for that matter, the elderly, and the handicapped) slow down a society bent on technological achievement, industrial production, and successful competition. The child-centered societies of the human past have thus given way in many parts of the world to adult-centered societies in which there is little room for children to participate.

Parents today surely may be attached to or may focus upon their children, but many parents are also torn between what they perceive is necessary for success in the modern world and what they perceive is necessary for their children. Schools in the United States reflect this confusion. They have been characterized as "holding tanks" where children may be taken care of, taught information and skills, given every opportunity — and kept out of the way.

THE TRIUMPH OF SELF-INTEREST

Membership in a group is no longer the automatic and obvious advantage it has always been in human life. In modern technological societies self-interest is not held in check by the need to belong to a community in order to survive. In fact, self-interest may be so well rewarded that it becomes disconnected from communal relationships and totally unbridled.

The size of modern societies and the divided allegiances that result make it possible for people to evade social responsibility rather easily. Cephu, a selfish Mbuti hunter described by Turnbull, sought to obtain a better catch for himself by putting his nets in advance of the other hunters. Discovery of his crime was inevitable, and he could not avoid the consequences of his transgression. For us, however, crime often pays.

In large societies it is possible to remain relatively anonymous in many areas of social activity and thus pursue one's ends with little interference from others. At the same time, since the criteria for acceptable behavior and skillful accomplishment in a modern society are so vague, it is possible to feign both social and personal competence without being discovered. If "nothing is hidden in the igloo" of the Netsilik Eskimo, a great deal may be hidden in the inner-city apartment or suburban home.

Finally, when wrongdoers are uncovered in a modern society, they are usually referred to an "authority," so that the people who have suffered at the hands of the offending individual are thoroughly separated from that individual's punishment. They too may evade responsibility in that they do not have to deal with the transgressor as an individual.

THE MALE-FEMALE IMBALANCE

Many of the changes that have had a significant impact on the development of individual identity and sense of self have taken place in the area of male-female relations and the division of labor. Though the sexual division of labor has persisted into modern times, the balances that characterized it in nomadic foraging societies have become disrupted. With the development of sedentary societies, the status of the activities traditionally engaged in by women has diminished significantly. In fact, it would be possible to write a history of civilization organized in terms of the accelerating erosion of the importance of the female dimension of experience in social structure and group decisionmaking. This erosion is related to other changes noted above: increased distance from the natural environment, large size and specialization, and the reduction of the central place of children in the life of the society. Regardless of its exact cause, this decline of the female dimension has resulted in an imbalance of such proportions that both men and women find it alarming and are greatly confused.

Not only has the balance itself been disrupted, but the entire framework through which males and females cooperated and through which each might obtain a different but equivalent status has broken down. Today there appears to be only one line of achievement that is recognized by both men and women. Women are constrained to discover their personal identity in terms described by male experience in the course of rather recent history. The impact of this breakdown on the environment of children's learning cannot be overemphasized. We have made it nearly impossible for girls to become women confidently or for boys confidently to become men.

THE SEGREGATION OF COGNITIVE AND EMOTIONAL PROCESSES

One of the most remarkable changes that has occurred in the development of large societies is the ever-increasing emphasis on cognitive activities that take place outside the context of subsistence and social life. This separation of cognitive skill from other areas of human endeavor—and particularly from the emotional systems that underlie social interaction— has had a significant effect on how modern society views children's learning and consequently on how children are educated.

The close connection between cognitive and emotional processes in small societies was clearly illustrated in a famous study by Jerome Bruner (1971) done among the Wolof in Senegal. Bruner gave Piagetian conservation tests to children who (1) were completely unschooled, (2) had attended village schools in rural areas, and (3) had gone to French schools in Dakar. Bruner saw that the performance of these children in the Piagetian tasks varied according to the amount of exposure to Western culture they had had and, specifically, to the amount and kind of schooling in which they had engaged. Wolof children who had been educated in French schools performed about as well as the European children tested originally by Piaget, while the Wolof children who had attended the bush schools or who had attended no school at all performed at progressively lower levels. Other findings by Price-Williams (1961) and DeLacey (1970, 1971) substantiate Bruner's claim that schooling and exposure have a signficant effect on the development of the ability to perform more sophisticated cognitive operations in the Piagetian hierarchy.

Bruner took these data as evidence that the Piagetian stages are more flexible than many child-development theorists had thought, but he discovered another difference between the unschooled and the schooled Wolof children that is far more interesting from an evolutionary point of view:

> In both the conservation and the concept experiments, the children were asked to give reasons for their answers. With both American and European children this type of question is usually put something like this: "Why do you say (or think) that thus and such is true?" Specifically, in a conservation problem, a child might be asked: "Why do you say that this glass has more water than this one?" But this type of a question would meet with uncomprehending silence when addressed to the unschooled [Wolof] children. If, however, the same question were changed in form to "Why *is* thus and such true?" it could often be answered quite easily. It would seem that the unschooled Wolof children lack Western self-consciousness: they do not distinguish between their own thought or statement about something and the thing itself. (1971, 25–26)

Wolof children who had been educated in the Western mode had developed a distance between the world and their perception of it, between reality and their view of reality. This self-consciousness represents an abstraction of cognitive processes that is very new in human experience. Most significantly for children's education in modern industrialized societies, the ability to dissociate one's thinking from the object of one's thought has not only become the most valued of a child's abilities but has become the very definition of intelligence.

The use made of children's cognitive capacity and the emotional relationship children have to their world may vary greatly between cultures (see Modgil 1974). The cultural bias of the Piagetian model (and others) has been examined rigorously in recent years, and many are beginning to believe that logico-mathematical reasoning, said by Piaget to be the highest form of cognitive activity, is not the only sophisticated intellectual operation of which humans are capable. According to Price-Williams,

> A mode of thought may exist which does in fact not sharply distinguish intellect and emotion, logic and rhetoric and so forth. It does not follow from this theory that such thought processes are primitive, nor that the people who adopt this thinking cannot adopt strict logical criteria when the situation warrants. . . . What seems to be at the bottom of the difficulty of understanding this type of thought is that "logic," "intellect," and "abstraction" are in fact terms which obey certain rules. We like to think that these rules fall along a continuum of development, both phylogenetic and ontogenetic. In addition, this path of development is regarded as unilineal, and any deviation from it perceived as inferior. Some people are now suspecting that parallel lines of development exist: that certain spheres of human activity require one kind of thinking, others demand other kinds of thinking, and each has its own set of rules. . . . Further suspicion arises that what has been hitherto demeaned as "primitive thinking" may indeed be quite sophisticated, and that the reason such thought has been labelled inferior is that we have no understanding of it. (1975, 82)

From this perspective the measurements of "intelligence" devised by psychometricians of one culture are merely a reflection of the *rules* of cognitive activity current in that culture rather than a true estimate of the *capacity* of a given individual or population to learn those (or any other) rules. Within a particular culture that makes particular cognitive demands (i.e., requires the intellect to function according to certain rules), these measurements may be valuable in that they can show whether individuals have learned the rules or not. But it is foolish to confuse these measurements with the capacity to learn rules.

Blurton Jones and Konner describe the sophistication of !Kung hunters in the formation and testing of hypotheses regarding animal behavior and suggest that "evolution has produced in them an inquisitive turn of mind which leads them to explore problems and accumulate knowledge beyond what it is more immediately necessary for them to know" (1976, 342).

Despite their analytical sophistication the !Kung, like the Wolof, would probably not understand a question that asked them to dissociate themselves from their environment — either physical or social. No doubt !Kung children would perform at a lower level on the Piagetian tests than European or American children. But if we could construct tests that measured a !Kung child's understanding of the trance dance or of n/um and the !kia state, we might be able to measure his or her "intelligence" more accurately.

It is likely that the basic cognitive equipment of the human being was developed in a context of daily problem solving and pattern perception that included the proposing and testing of hypotheses. But these patterns and problems always occurred in a framework that consisted of the ancient emotional systems associated with belonging to a group, being important as an individual in that group, and exploring the environment.

The extraordinary ability of the human intellect segregated from other human characteristics is what we teach and praise in our schools. The ability to do abstract thinking has made it possible for humans to create astounding miracles of technology, art, and thought. In the process of technological invention and conceptual creation, we have totally geared the formal education of our children to their cognitive abilities (as measured by the tests). We have challenged them with abstraction and have inundated them with information. This kind of education has made it possible for some children to make extraordinary achievements. In teaching children this way, however, we have ignored the fundamental connection between cognitive skill and emotional need. We have isolated the intellectual capacity from the context in which it evolved and in which it has had its most significant meaning throughout human history. It is irresponsible to think that no consequences are associated with this split. They may, in fact, be observed in the scholar, full of information and adept at cognitive abstraction, who does not know how to behave in a social group and believes that knowing how to behave is not important.

SKILLS AND ATTITUDES FOR CHANGE
AND FRAGMENTATION

Children's learning is affected by biologically based needs, yet we neither can nor would wish to go back to the nomadic foraging way of life.

Dealing effectively with a modern technological environment obviously requires new skills and attitudes. What are they, and how are they connected or disconnected with ancient human needs?

Change and Speed   The encounter with accelerating change is crucial to the identification of these new skills and attitudes, not only because so much has changed but because the *expectation* and the *acceptance* of change from generation to generation is a totally new dimension of human experience (Mead 1970). And to the perception of and accommodation to change must be added the perception of and accommodation to speed, to the sheer velocity of any activity—any movement between thoughts, circumstances, perceptions, or foci of attention.

Change is an integral part of technological culture. We have also seen that change itself can undermine security and bring anxiety (note the "Social Readjustment Rating Scale" developed by T. H. Holmes and R. N. Rahe 1967). To add to the confusion, we have to some extent accepted the fact that, if children do not acquire attributes that are connected with understanding, tolerating, and preparing for change, they will be unable to obtain either security or status in the world. Thus it is not surprising to see a growing respect in United States society for attributes such as "flexibility" and "tolerance for ambiguity," even though such qualities are often superimposed upon older social attributes such as "firmness of purpose" or "loyalty," with which they may at times seem to be at odds. "Going with the flow" is said to be different from being "weak and wishy-washy," though the line of demarcation is anybody's guess. Surely "rolling with the punches" in a modern society buys a little time to sort out the shifting characteristics of a particular problem or encounter (or at least allows one to wait with less anxiety while they sort themselves out). Being flexible reserves one's energy and enables one to avoid heavy emotional or physical investment in something that may prove to be ephemeral. It might be said, in fact, that attributes such as flexibility and tolerance for ambiguity are vital if an individual is to maintain any sense of continuity or meaning in a society changing as rapidly as ours is.

Information Processing and Abstraction   Another new dimension of experience in a modern, industrial society is the existence of vast quantities of information, accumulated over more than five thousand years and generated today at an ever-increasing rate. It is impossible for any individual to absorb, or even have access to, more than an infinitesimal fraction of this whole, and surely part of the ambiguity that we must learn to tolerate originates in the insecurity of our irredeemable ignorance. This ignorance is all the more disquieting because there is every reason to believe that much of this Information That We Cannot Know is vital. It serves as the basis for decisions that affect our lives profoundly but are made by others.

In the age of the information glut, it is important for people not only to learn to read, write, listen well, and do math but also to develop abstracting and organizing skills. It is not enough to analyze information; one must be able to systematize it too. In the absence of a common framework within which information is interpreted, such as existed in nomadic foraging societies, we will be overwhelmed by the sheer quantity unless we know how to make connections and design intellectual categories, recognize patterns and relationships, and prioritize them. All normally developed humans have the capacity to perform these cognitive tasks to some degree, but as the amount of information that must be organized increases, the intellectual processes involved become increasingly abstract, divorced from the experience of individuals and from emotional need.

Is it not possible that like the rhesus macaques described by Lewis and Sackett (see above, p. 27) our "willingness to perform" may be greatly diminished in such an environment? As with flexibility and tolerance of ambiguity, the need for new abstracting skills is coexistent with the anxiety that is produced by our inability to catch up and by the linearity of abstraction itself. Perhaps it is true that, increasingly, "successful" individuals in American life are those who can respond effectively and with minimal anxiety to change and who are able to organize information rapidly into useful categories. For others, however, the anxiety is overwhelming. Whether one is effective or anxious is usually a matter of luck or opportunity rather than innate ability.

In the face of ever-increasing specialization, it is hard to belong anywhere genuinely, and it is often easier simply to "find a niche" than to develop broad organizing and synthesizing skills. Perhaps it is in part this very response that makes it possible for a highly specialized and fragmented society to continue to function and to specialize and fragment even further. Unfortunately, this tendency is easily taken advantage of, and a new "skill" that lends itself to the maintenance of a highly specialized and compartmentalized society is the skill of *obedience*.

Members of foraging bands are never obedient in the sense that we use the term. Adults do not recognize an unquestionable authority in leaders, nor do children recognize such authority in their parents. But people who are buried in inaccessible information, frozen in specialities, and required to manipulate abstract categories in order to understand the world around them may find obedience an important survival technique. Obedience, of course, can assuage the anxiety of unknowing.

Heightened Competition and New Kinds of Self-Reliance   Competition is muted in nomadic foraging societies, but it forms a behavioral and philosophical cornerstone of modern industrial society, regardless of political ideology. In the United States, for example, competitiveness demands a certain willingness to take a chance, to risk losing—a new form of self-reliance. The skills of winning and losing in our society range from an ability to assess risk to dogged determination, unconscious talent, and ruthless immorality. In our time, working around or outside the rules is a skill that, like flexibility, is receiving more and more attention and respect.

But even as flexibility may at times contradict another important social attribute such as loyalty, the skills of successful competition are often in opposition to the need of even a highly fragmented society for cooperation. Self-reliance is an important characteristic of individuals in nomadic foraging societies, but that self-reliance is, as we have seen, located in an all-pervasive social context. In our society self-reliance is simply laid over the need for reliance on others, and there is rarely an integration of the two because reciprocity itself has been abstracted and quantified. Although competition is encouraged in the schools, cooperation is encouraged too. Children are taught the value of team play even as they are urged, first, to measure their abilities against those of their teammates and, second, to beat the opposing team at all costs. The skills and attitudes of competition and the skills and attitudes of cooperation are often taught jumbled together indiscriminately, so that the predominant communication to children must be confusion and uncertainty.

Getting used to change, to the dynamics of abstraction and overwhelming masses of information, and to the demands of competition are not the only modifications that have been required of the human species in technological societies. But there is no doubt that the skills and attitudes we need to do these things well represent unfamiliar territory for us all. We are coerced by the inexorability and obvious speed of change into accepting and expecting it, though for most of our past we perceived and expected none. We are inundated with perpetually novel information that is critical to our well-being but is beyond our reach either because it is simply impossible for us absorb it or because we do not have access to it. We are urged toward specialization at increasingly early stages of life, so that today's high school students often major in subject areas before they have any concept of how one subject relates to another.

Formal education is in a difficult position, for we have asked the schools to do more than pass on the skills of reading, writing, and computing and the history and values of the culture. We want them to keep up with every change as well. The same parents who insist that their children learn a generalized obedience to adults in school also insist that their children's schooling lead to successful employment.

The need for cooperation does not disappear in an environment that increasingly rewards self-interest and -reliance; the expectation of change does not supplant the expectation of continuity and security. Parents want the schools to prepare children for life in the modern world and at the same time keep them true to the "basic" principles of the culture—even though there is less and less agreement concerning the identity of these principles.

Great changes have taken place in the learning environment since the advent of large societies, and children in modern industrial societies have real needs for intellectual skills that help them cope with change, information, and competition. At the same time, however, children in all nations on earth are still motivated to learn by ancient socioemotional needs and by a native curiosity that urges them to investigate the physical and social world. In United States society the school has taken on an increasing role in the preparation of children for adult life, and in the next chapter we will examine such a school environment from an evolutionary perspective.

9

Learning in the Schools

I N the environment of a typical public school in the United States, children's biologically based needs simultaneously to belong to a group, to challenge the group, and to explore everything in the world are likely to be frustrated at a fairly early age. The negative characteristics of schooling have been noted many times by many observers, but if we locate these characteristics in the context of our socioemotional learning heritage, we may see them in a new light.

One of the most important issues that emerges from this view concerns the relationship between children's learning needs and schooling as a preparation for adult life in the "much changed environment" described in the last chapter. Dreeben (1968) believes that the school fulfills an important function for children as a transition between family relationships and the less personal, more competitive relationships of the adult world. In school, according to Dreeben, children learn the skills and attitudes associated with independence, achievement, the existence of organizational rules, and the fragmentation or specificity that reduces interaction to a narrow range. If these new characteristics are required in contemporary adult society, would not an attempt to address children's biologically based needs actually do them a disservice?

This complicated issue involves not only the function of the school but also the legitimacy of the society for which children are supposed to be prepared. In this chapter and in the rest of part 3, these issues will surface again and again: Must socialization in a modern industrial culture work against children's natural inclinations and needs to be successful? If not, how may we change the environment of the school? If so, what may we learn about our society from the way we treat our children?

ATTACHMENT, BELONGING, AND COOPERATION

Children bring with them to school a need to belong and to be close, but the very size of many schools and of individual classes within schools makes it difficult or impossible for children to fulfill this need. American schools have grown in size steadily throughout their history for a variety of reasons that are perfectly logical in terms of perceived cultural needs. It has been argued, for example, that large schools are more efficient, that they are cheaper, that they expose children to a larger cross-section of society, that the efficiency of size makes it possible to provide a larger number of children with sophisticated equipment, and so forth. So persuasive have these arguments been that today in many parts of the country there are public schools serving more than four thousand students. The socialization problems associated with large classes have been obvious for twenty years (see Jackson 1968), but from an evolutionary perspective one of the most serious problems of large classes and schools is that there is little opportunity for children to have a sense of belonging in such communities assuming that the need to belong is best fulfilled in band-sized, egalitarian groups.

Of course, large size also implies standardization, elaborate rules and regulations, and rigid scheduling (see Callahan 1962; Jackson 1968). Collecting four thousand children together in the same facility will indeed make it possible to expose all of them to sophisticated learning environments and materials such as well-equipped biology labs and computers. But so many children cannot use these facilities all at once, which means that they cannot use them in a way and at a time they devise themselves. Exposure must be scheduled so that all will get a turn, and a formal curriculum must be drawn up in terms of a "scope and sequence" of skills, or "behavioral objectives," so that all will have the same kind of experience with the equipment.

This relationship between size and standardization is as evident on the level of the individual class as it is on the level of the school or school system. Many of the rules imposed on the behavior of, say, a sixth-grade class of thirty children do not derive from the needs of children as much as from the sheer impossibility of dealing with thirty children of the same age any other way. Large size alone thus makes it virtually impossible for children to determine where and how they belong to the group (whatever group it is) in the ways that best suit this discovery. Impossible numbers alone make the school an artificial learning environment by evolutionary standards.

The relative exclusion of children's families from the life of the school makes matters even worse. Parents are often marginally involved in their children's education; they may be members of the PTA, may serve on the school board, or may take an interest in their children's homework. But parents are seldom part of the day-to-day social interactions of a public school in any significant way. They really never know firsthand what their children are learning in school or how they behave. Furthermore, they are unable to assess accurately the quality of the social environment or the appropriateness of the adult models presented to children by teachers. Parents receive most, if not all, of their information about the school secondhand—either from children or from administrators and teachers, who have vested interests to protect.

As children grow older and go to larger and larger schools, their ability to participate as full members of the group that is formed by the institution rapidly diminishes. Elementary school children have a much better chance of satisfying their need to belong than junior high or high school students. In typical elementary schools children usually have a single main teacher for the entire year. They have a home base, their room, which they can decorate with their own creations. Elementary schools are usually much smaller than junior high schools or high schools and are more likely to be located in neighborhoods, so that young children are often in school with other children who are their friends outside of school. At the same time children in elementary schools are more likely to be encouraged to try everything rather than specialize.

Compared with the intense closeness and sense of attachment and security that characterize nomadic foraging societies, social involvement in the elementary school is pretty weak. But being in an elementary school is like being in a hunting-and-gathering band compared with what comes next.

At the age of eleven or twelve, children in public education move from elementary schools to junior high schools. Suddenly a child on the verge of puberty is placed in unfamiliar territory, with a new selection of peers and new teachers who have new, increasingly abstract expectations. One of the most confusing aspects of this change from an elementary school to a junior high school is the way in which the day is broken into small pieces that seem to have no relation to one another. Hundreds of thousands of children in the United States start their day in *homeroom* (an interesting term from an evolutionary perspective) and then proceed in fifty-minute intervals to English, gym, history, lunch, Spanish, and so forth. These specialized, short-term learning environments provide few or no clues that help children get a sense of the relationship between the chunks of information being imparted to them in each environment—much less help them see a relationship between what they are feeling as adolescents and what they are getting in class. As John Holt says, "In many ways, we break down children's convictions that things make sense, or their hope that things may prove to make sense. We do it, first of all, by breaking up life into arbitrary and disconnected chunks of subject matter, which we then try to 'integrate' by . . . artificial and irrelevent devices" (1964, 209).

If this approach to learning does prepare children for the "real world," it prepares them to be confused and to be content with confusion. It surely does not prepare them to organize their perceptions or give them the confidence to look for meaning.

The fragmentation of subject matter is only one effect of the specialization that breaks up closeness and community in the public schools. The identification of teachers and school administrators as "experts in education" tends to intimidate many parents who might otherwise become more involved in their children's formal learning. And as the schools have taken on more and more of the socialization of young people in United States society, a great breach has opened between home and school. In a similar way specialization often separates school administrators from teachers and some teachers from other teachers. An excellent example of this problem is the split between vocational teachers and academic teachers in a trade school.

Reciprocity in a foraging band is ensured by a variety of relationships and conventions that tie individuals together and motivate cooperation.

No such relations or traditions exist in the school, except in the most attenuated and abstracted forms. For the most part the "exchange" relationships of a public school are one-sided and coercive: for obeying the teachers and fulfilling the requirements of each class, children get good grades, teacher approval, and parental reinforcement.

Of course children are resourceful and resilient (see Giroux 1983). They form their own groups, which can provide some of the needed intimacy and which resist to some extent the isolating processes of the school. But these groups also tend to be isolated from and even antagonistic toward one another. Cliques, gangs, and clubs form, and these groups often draw their identity more from a sense of who or what they are *not* than of who they are. In addition, the groups children form on their own are often treated as subversive by adults (no doubt because they often are). Then, of course, some children are left out. They have no group and live in perpetual anxiety.

PLACE, STATUS, AND IDENTITY

In a public school, children have very little control over their time or the direction of their energy and attention (see Boocock 1980 and Hurn 1985 for sociological overviews of power relationships in the schools). Activities are usually closely scheduled, and children have virtually no say regarding when certain activities are engaged in, much less whether they will engage in them or not. A child who is hungry must wait until lunchtime. A child with high energy, who would normally be running it off outside, must wait until recess. A child who has to go to the bathroom must have a pass. As noted many times in the literature critical of public schools (e.g., Holt 1964; Silberman 1970; Henry 1963), all the power in a school flows one way—from the teachers and administrators downward to the children.

One of the most complicated obstacles for children to overcome is the manner in which schools narrow the range of acceptable knowledge and skill and form them into hierarchies. All children acquire a considerable repertoire of skills and an extensive library of knowledge before they ever set foot in a school, and long after they begin school children retain respect for a wide range of abilities in one another. The child who can jump rope well acquires a certain status within the group, as does the child who can whistle, ride a bike, or draw. But once children arrive at school, they are rewarded primarily for (1) intellectual skills connected with the acquisition and repetition of increasingly abstract information and (2) social skills that make life easier for the adults (e.g., getting along with others, keeping quiet, obeying). There is little opportunity for children to demonstrate or receive credit for other abilities they may have. Over time, an official hierarchy of skill and knowledge, fostered by teachers and administrators (and, usually, parents), is grudgingly accepted by the children.

For young children, reading well, memorizing multiplication tables, and keeping quiet may not be particularly important achievements. Other things may attract their attention more forcefully. But the hierarchical valuation of skill, a pillar of the institutional learning environment, results in an inevitable constriction of status possibilities. By the time an adolescent reaches high school, there are great gulfs of status between, for example, vocational skills and academic skills, or between children who are in a college-preparation course of study and those who are in a general program. Although there are exceptions, such as athletic achievement, it is fair to say that, in general, adults esteem most highly those children with the best-developed academic skills. This hierarchy leaves its mark on everyone who goes through public schooling in the United States.

Thus, in whatever way the status of an individual child in school reflects the stratum of society from which he or she comes, social hierarchy is exacerbated by the "culture of education." Not only are the subject areas of formal education specialized, but education itself is a specialty, and many of the values that are imposed upon the environment of the school are educational values such as doing well on tests, reading well, writing well, doing math, being cooperative with teachers, and so on. In the world of the school, making a fine piece of furniture does not count for as much as doing well on a geography test.

Teachers may surely be forgiven for their attempts to "professionalize" their work, given their own low status in the culture (Boocock 1980). But a side effect of this professionalization is the creation of a subculture with values and expectations that are often very different from those in a child's family. The net result of such an environment, in spite of the best intentions, is often anxiety and confusion for the child and intimidation of parents. Indeed, the discontinuities between the educational sub-culture and the culture at large may help to account for the fact that almost *everybody* is dissatisfied with what the schools are doing.

A serious problem with the way children achieve identity and impor-tance in school involves competition. Personal achievement is usually measured in terms of how one does *in comparison with* others. This fact is evident in a system of evaluation that involves hierarchical grades.

The detrimental effects of grading on children's learning have been noted:

> One may wonder whether the present system of rewards and punish-ments as seen by pupils in school actually tends to inhibit the use of intuitive thinking. The assignment of grades in school typically emphasizes the acquisition of factual knowledge primarily because that is what is most easily evaluated; moreover, it tends to em-phasize the correct answer, since it is the correct answer on the straightforward examination that can be graded as "correct." (Bruner 1977, 66)

Grading further constricts the ways in which a child may be acknowl-edged—especially by school adults and parents—and pits children against one another in the most artificial and destructive way. For all the problems of organized athletics in school, in a team sport a child may at least learn cooperation and respect for others and may know the pleasure of mastering a skill. But the competition fostered on report-card day when one child asks another "What did you get?" has no redeeming features.

If well-being for humans includes a sense of personal identity and status, we must acknowledge that, in institutions of formal education, we are conditioning children to get used to life without a full sense of self. Children are being taught to find compensations for, or to ignore, needs that are deeply rooted in human biology. For some this compensa-tion may take the form of subordination to the directives of adults in the school (and by extension to other authorities in the society). For others, "success" in school allows a certain status in the culture at large. From an evolutionary perspective, it is easy to see why those who have acquired status so often internalize the values of the institution that has made such a positive experience possible (see Bowles and Gintis 1976). For others, the sense of powerlessness and anonymity that comes from having the need for status and personal identity thwarted results in violence, drug abuse, apathy, and mental if not physical dissociation from the life of the school. Jules Henry recognized the seriousness of depriving children of a free hand in the acquisition of personal status more than twenty years ago.

> Now, if children are taught to adopt alienation as a way of life, it follows that they must have feelings of inadequacy, for nothing so saps self-confidence as alienation from the Self. It would follow that school, the chief agent in the process, must try to provide the children with "ego support," for culture tries to remedy the ills it creates.
>
> Hence the effort to give recognition. . . . That anything essential was nurtured in this way is an open question, for the kind of individuality that was recognized as the children picked titles out of the [songbook] index was mechanical, without a creative dimension, and under the strict control of the teacher. Let us conclude this discussion by saying that school metamorphoses the child, giving it the kind of Self the school can manage, and then proceeds to minister to the Self it has made. (1963, 291–92)

THE ATTENTION STRUCTURE IN THE SCHOOLS

Male-Female Roles and Relations   The gross imbalance between the values accorded male experience and female experience in our society and the anxiety this imbalance produces are reflected in the schools and still are often perpetuated there. Not surprisingly, the gender roles presented to boys and girls in the schools are usually abstractions of the already abstracted roles that exist for men and women in the larger society.

The presentation of gender roles to children in United States society— in the media, for example—has become so ridiculous and at the same time so damaging that educators across the country have urged the development of a "nonsexist" education in which boys and girls are educated from the perspective not of difference but of similarity. To the extent that nonsexist education attempts to restore value and meaning to the female experience, it is a laudable effort. From an evolutionary perspective, however, we see that children may be more confused than empowered and enlightened by an environment in which males and females are presented as being the same.

The problem is not that gender roles in the United States are different but that they are, for the most part, *meaningless*, both in terms of whether the functions defined by the roles may best be performed by males or females and in terms of the reciprocal relations that different roles for males and females are supposed to ensure. Worse, these roles are often impossible for boys and demeaning for girls, so that relations between the sexes are poisoned by uneasy expectations all around. Though most children are motivated by ancient emotions to enter into reciprocal relationships with members of the opposite sex about the time they reach puberty, the *vision* of that relationship children actually acquire from society is far from reciprocal, and the vision that children acquire from non-sexist education is disorienting.

The Adult Context   In a modern industrial society all adults with whom a child comes in contact are, so to speak, lacking in depth. Adults are unidimensional figures who fill particular, specialized roles and offer children foci for attention that are flat, unreal, and often uninteresting. The child rarely, if ever, sees adults responding to a variety of situations or playing a number of roles. In the eyes of children, adults are retail clerks, teachers, ministers, nurses, and so forth. Even within the family, the parents' work (the activities that command such a great amount of *their* energy and attention) is often mysterious to children.

Nowhere in the experience of children in modern industrial society is this fragmentation and specialization of the meaning of adult life more obvious than in the schools. And this situation has a negative effect on both the children and the adults involved. To begin with, there is no real connection between the world of the family and the world of the school, and the adult roles children *do* see their parents play usually have nothing to do with the adult roles they see their teachers and other school personnel play.

The school environment prepares students primarily for the school environment, as Jules Henry said, and for a very abstracted concept of adult life. Within the school the adults with whom children come in contact serve as highly specialized models for adult behavior. From this perspective it is not remarkable that children who do well in school (i.e., achieve status and acquire a certain scholarly identity) and have the opportunity to do so stay in school as long as they can.

Judgments of worth, of attractiveness, and of meaning are made by children on the basis of what they *see* adults around them doing, not on the basis of what the adults tell them should be worthy, attractive, or meaningful. In nomadic foraging societies the adults are visible to the children in many roles and in many varied situations, and this panorama of moods, reactions, and competencies offers children a model of adulthood that is complex, interesting, and variable. But the relationships between children and adults in the modern school almost *guarantee* confusion and boredom for both. Adults in the schools are able to perform only specific functions, often on a child's level, for most of their working day, and it is not surprising that their interest soon flags. The children can easily sense the resulting attitudes of boredom and routinization.

Children spend their first sixteen to eighteen years observing the fragmented activities of their parents, their teachers, and all the other adults around them. Then, suddenly, whether at sixteen years of age for a high school dropout, eighteen for a high school graduate, or twenty-one for a college graduate, children are expected to begin filling adult roles for which they have supposedly been preparing in school. The transition to adulthood in United States society is regularly traumatic, for children soon discover as they search for jobs and wrestle with responsibility that they have been prepared for roles that either do not really exist in the society or exist only in the artificial environment of institutions such as the school.

This insight is part of the answer to the issue discussed at the beginning of this chapter. If, indeed, children were being prepared to be competent adults by the confusion, competitiveness, and fragmentation of the school environment, the evolutionary critique might be tempered. The adult world as presented to children in the schools, however, does not provide a consistent or integrated focus of attention for children's development. Nor does it serve as a model of adult reality. Perhaps the critical importance of children's peer groups in modern industrial societies—not only as environments for learning but as definers of identity and arbiters of meaning as well—is related to this fragmentation of the adult world as seen by children (see Coleman 1961).

Other Children   Students in school are segregated by age to such an extent that the mixed-age groupings that occur naturally in foraging societies are impossible. To be sure, many children have some contact with others of different ages within their own families and in their neighborhoods, but for the time they are in school, they are usually separated from both older and younger children. In addition, children transfer age segregation from the school to the neighborhood, often refusing to play with those who are younger or older.

A world in which children are categorized according to age and grade is highly artificial, and children's gradual perception of these segregations and hierarchies as normal makes it all the more difficult for them to learn normally. As in nomadic foraging societies 500,000 years ago, so in today's neighborhoods: much of the important learning that small children do comes through watching and imitating older children.

By the same token, all higher primates, and especially humans, need a certain amount of practice in order to become competent parents. Surely the schools are contributing to modern confusion about child rearing by fixing children from the age of five or younger in an environment in which they are always with age-mates. Older children do not get the opportunities to observe and interact with younger children and infants— experiences that will give them valuable information and practice for their own parenting.

Unnatural Discipline   Children are curious beings who are predisposed to investigate their environment. In the schools, however, instead of being able to follow their natural predispositions to investigate the environment on their own terms, children are compelled to follow a set of rigid rules designed for the convenience of adults. Children's curiosity, their responses to novelty, and their motivation to explore are too intemperate for a school. The modern educational environment—large in size, isolated from family life, specialized and segregated—cannot tolerate anything like the full range of learning styles and activities that constitute the human evolutionary heritage.

Children in school are trained over the years to direct their attention on command, to focus on math when it is time for math, on history when it is time for history, and so forth. Although the ability to concentrate and direct one's attention at will is an important information-age processing skill, the focus on external rather than internal motivations in the school often does considerable damage. If children are unable to explore their world and exercise their curiosity in ways that allow *them* to control their investment of time and energy, they may learn to stop exploring — particularly if they are punished for not making their investigations at acceptable times and in acceptable ways. Such children may seek refuge in obedience, as noted above, or may simply seek to escape the constricted environment of the school as soon as possible.

HOW CHILDREN LEARN IN SCHOOL

The specific activities through which children acquire information and gain competence in a gathering-and-hunting society are appropriate to the knowledge and skill they need to be well-functioning adults in their society. But in public schools in the United States, learning does not discernibly relate to the significant aspects of adult life. Is it any wonder that children so often ask the question, "Why do we have to do this?"

For many years rote memorization was the predominant mode of learning, particularly in the higher grades. The emphasis was on the acquisition of information that flowed from teacher to student or from book to student and was then repeated by the student so that his or her acquisition of the information could be evaluated. If the way humans learn language is an apt metaphor for the way children in nomadic foraging societies learn most of what they need to know, the way children in the United States learn the multiplication tables symbolizes much of the overall approach to learning that has been characteristic of American public education over the years — that is, memorization of abstract information that is not connected with the child's personal experience, fragmentation and specialization of subject matter, repetition of information, and evaluation based on the child's ability to produce what the teacher demands.

In recent years, educators have made significant attempts to reduce the amount of memorization children have to do, to integrate better the subject matter presented to children, and to foster thinking skills rather than repeating skills. These palliatives alone, however, are insufficient to the task because they are *intellectual* reforms only. In an effort to integrate reading and mathematics, for example, children are given word problems in arithmetic. But these are not the children's problems; they originate in the minds of adults who are attempting to convey what is still an abstract body of knowledge and to think like children.

The fragmentation of children's social relationships in the schools is surely exacerbated by the activities of learning. Children are told to "be silent" in the classroom, to "do their own work," even though they are constantly motivated internally to talk, to engage one another, and to explore the classroom and the world outside. Consider Silberman's example:

> ITEM: The report card that a well-to-do suburban school system uses for kindergartners grades the five-year-olds on their "readiness for First Grade Work." Readiness involves some seventeen attributes, the first three of which read as follows:
>   1. Sits still and works at assigned task for 15 to 20 minutes.
>   2. Listens and follows direction.
>   3. Displays good work habits. (1970, 130)

Most classrooms — especially at the junior and senior high levels — are arranged with rows of chairs facing the teacher, and though observation and listening skills are encouraged, they are usually encouraged only in their passive form and within the framework set by the teacher, the curriculum, or the schedule. More active investigation, experimentation, or play (much less, certain unflattering imitations) are rigorously discouraged in school.

Ironically, most subjects in the schools are connected *only* by the modes in which they are presented to children and in the ways children must engage them. There is really little difference between the way in which children learn about American history and the way in which they learn about algebra. There is typically little attempt in the public schools to match content and process. On the contrary, an attempt is made to standardize the activities and the outcomes of learning as much as possible. This trend may be discerned in the ways in which educational technology such as teaching machines and computers has been used in the schools in recent years.

In this chapter I have tried to reveal the seriousness of the gap that exists between the ways in which children learn inevitably and the environment and activities of learning in a modern public school. In the next chapter I present a set of evolutionary principles that can guide the development of a school appropriate to children's learning needs.

10

Creating the Appropriate School

HOW may an evolutionary perspective on human learning be applied to children's formal education? In this chapter I present certain principles that follow from this perspective. These principles concern:

evaluation of educational processes and programs
the size of schools and learning groups
power and participation of children in their own learning
the way in which various skills are valued
adult models for children's learning
other children and the elderly

Difficult questions are associated with the implementation of these principles, and before describing them I would like to offer a kind of case study of one such question: can we help boys and girls acquire an appropriate gender identity, one that offers a clear picture of maleness and femaleness without contributing to inequality?

From the study of other primate societies and nomadic foraging societies it is clear that differences between the ways males and females experience and understand the world (and are motivated to behave in it) go back to the beginning of our species and beyond. From an evolutionary perspective, differences in male and female experience are biologically based and are therefore of critical importance to a child's sense of self.

If one analyzed male-female relations no further, it would be easy enough to justify current gender roles in the United States. In much the same way, Herbert Spencer used Darwin's ideas to justify the status of the British Empire in his time. It could be said, for example, on the basis of this simplistic perspective, that, since a woman's sphere of experience has always revolved around the bearing and rearing of children, a woman's place—even in the Information Age—is still in the home.

But from a broader evolutionary perspective, this view is foolish. While the differences between men and women are very important, they are important only because they have ensured cooperation, sharing, survival, and equality throughout our history as a species. During most of human existence the differences between men and women made it possible for both to survive more effectively in a given environment, to be full participants in a group, and, at the same time, to obtain individual status and importance. It is obvious that the differences between the experiences of men and women in the modern world perpetuate inequality rather than equality, and far from contributing to cooperation among people, they tend to provoke confusion, isolation, and rage.

For the educator trying to apply an evolutionary perspective in, say, the development of curriculum or pedagogy at school, there is a complex dilemma here. Male-female differences are rooted deeply in human biology, so an educational program that attempts to make boys and girls equal by constraining them to have the same experiences (or forcing them to interpret their experiences in the same way) will cause problems. Such an education could be dangerous to a child's sense of self. On the other hand, it is clearly harmful, again from an evolutionary perspective, to socialize boys and girls into roles and self-perceptions that perpetuate imbalance and inequality.

Some might say that the educator's problem is unresolvable. In a time when the differences between males and females no longer contribute to cooperation and equality, either the differences must be willfully erased or the inequalities must persist. But we need not be stuck on either horn of this dilemma. It is also possible to understand the differences between men and women in new ways that can again generate the dynamic social balances that characterized the human evolutionary past. The work of Carol Gilligan (1982), for example, describes an experience of life for women that is very different from men's. At the same time, Gilligan shows that this experience is every bit as valuable—to women and to society—as men's experience.

It seems possible to develop an education for children that validates the differences between males and females without denigrating the experience of either. If, as Gilligan says, female moral development tends to revolve around the perception and maintenance of interpersonal relationships and networks, while male moral development tends to revolve more around abstract principles (as shown in Kohlberg 1969), why not design educational activities for children that use both approaches to problem solving and demonstrate the value of each. Of course we have a great deal more to learn before we can develop curriculum along these lines with any confidence, but here are two examples of how evolutionary principles might be applied.

Games in our society are traditionally rule driven and highly competitive—elements, many believe, of male experience. Girls who want to participate in these activities are often constrained to imitate boys' experiences. But when my ten-year-old daughter plays Monopoly with her friends, the girls trade money and property around so that everyone can stay in the game. The rules are broken time and again in these games, but personal relationships are made stronger and become better defined. In the schools could we not support the kinds of games that have as their goal the involvement of children and the development of interpersonal networks? We should not simply force boys and girls to play noncompetitive games together. But the school can help make the case for a relational perspective to boys, who often dismiss girls' games, and for the advantages of rule-governed competition to girls, who often dismiss boys' games. The goal should be not to eradicate differences but to foster understanding of and respect for difference.

Traditional math instruction is another area that appears to favor boys over girls. Tobias (1978) and others have shown that, at higher levels of math, girls are not encouraged by teachers to achieve. But from an evolutionary perspective the problem of female math anxiety has as much to do with the highly individualized approach to problem solving in the schools as with gender roles and styles actively presented to children by teachers. Cognitive-style research (see Witkin 1973; Kagan, Moss, and Sigel 1963; Messick 1976) has shown that the *field-independent* style, characterized by an ability to extract and analyze elements of a problem according to rules, is far more common in males. The *field-dependent* style, however, which is more holistic, global, and relational, is more common in females. Field-independent instruction and expectations such as those that exist in a typical math class discriminate against a field-dependent approach. An evolutionary perspective helps us see that the gender-specific characteristics of field dependence and field independence, noted repeatedly in cognitive-style research, are not simply accidents of socialization in a particular culture. This view also urges support for a range of problem solving techniques and styles in the school. Why is it so important that children "do their own work" in school? Why may we not support group problem solving in math (and in other areas, for that matter), which favors a relational, interpersonal approach?

The answers are not easy, and the complexity of an evolutionary perspective may seem distressing at first. But an evolutionary perspective does offer certain principles that can guide us toward more inclusive, more equitable answers than those we have accepted in the past.

HUMANIZED CRITERIA FOR EVALUATION IN EDUCATION

An understanding of evolution in children's education can lead to expanding the criteria for evaluating both educational programs and the performance of children in these programs. For too many years, education in the United States has been evaluated on the basis of quantitative measurements alone, and most decisions about how education should be funded and structured have been made on the basis of these measurements. The following criteria should be added to quantitative evaluations of children's performance and school effectiveness:

1. the extent to which children have an understanding of the ways of the groups they belong to as a result of their educational experiences

2. the extent to which individual children are empowered by their educational experiences to influence decisions that are made concerning them

3. the extent to which children make an investment in the learning

process itself; that is, the enthusiasm and willingness to learn that they demonstrate

The numbers game in education dominates the decision-making processes currently employed by legislators, school committees, school administrators, teachers, parents, and, inevitably, the children themselves. It is unlikely that these quantitative measurements will ever be replaced by other criteria for evaluation, but we must balance our quantitative assessments with an understanding of the social impact of the school environment.

An evaluation of the achievement of individual children using these additional criteria naturally implies a similar evaluation of the schools themselves. If a child does not have an understanding of the way in which his or her group operates, perhaps it is because the group itself is ill defined and incomprehensible. If individual children are *not* making demands and pressing for attention, then perhaps they are oppressed. And if children have ceased to feel enthusiasm for learning, perhaps it is because the way they have been constrained to learn in school has no meaning for them.

QUESTIONS OF SIZE

A second principle that may be derived from an evolutionary perspective is that questions of size in the learning environment can never be reduced to questions of system efficiency, the sophistication of educational materials, or the competence of teachers. The larger the learning group, the more it must be managed; the pull toward structure, regularity, and predictability is irresistible. In general, the larger the number of children in a school group, the less opportunity these children will have to satisfy the need to belong to and be important in that group. To be sure, children will form their own groups, as noted in chapter 9, but neither the junior high school English class nor the junior high school itself can serve as a meaningful community to most youngsters if it is large.

One might point out that many children have perfectly positive experiences in large schools. It is important to note, however, that these experiences most often take place not in the context of the whole school or even the whole class but in small subgroups such as reading circles, sports teams, clubs, or school plays.

A small group makes it possible for children to assume more self-management, in Dewey's sense of the term, than a large group can allow. And small groups can create opportunities for children to help determine the quality and quantity of their participation in group activities. Because less management is required on the part of the teacher in a small group, the possibility of children's discovering or inventing on their own is enhanced.

In small learning groups greater diversity can be tolerated than in large, tightly managed groups, and this fact is of particular importance in a huge, pluralistic society. In foraging bands all the members of the group are seen by one another as unique individuals. The size of the band makes this familiarity possible. The same might be said for a learning group of young children. In groups of, say, fifteen to eighteen, it is almost impossible for children to see classmates of different races, religions or ethnic backgrounds as undimensional representatives of classes. Of course, the larger the group, the more easily stereotypes may be applied.

Size is not the only factor that affects the quality and effectiveness of the learning environment, but it is an important one. Children *will* be members of small groups in order to get what they need out of social life — whether these groups are sanctioned by adults or not. If educators and community members realize that the schools are already engaged in large-scale socialization, they will do well to consider how small communities may be fostered in the school. Naturally, this responsibility extends to school boards and to state and federal funding agencies, which need to review their assumptions about how many children a single teacher can handle in a class.

Many schools in the country have experimented with smaller alternative groups within the large school structure (see Raywid 1981), but an evolutionary perspective makes it clear that these exceptions should become the rule. A small class will be able to answer a wider range of human needs for a greater diversity of children than will a large class. A small school will be more accessible than a large school as a community to which children and parents alike may belong. There is no way to fudge this perception with more efficient structure, more sophisticated equipment, or better-trained teachers. In all educational decisions the size of the learning group should be a critical factor.

POWER AND PARTICIPATION OF CHILDREN

Size is such an important variable in the evaluation and planning of educational environments because it is characteristic of human learning for children to be powerful participants in the learning process. Many have observed the developmental importance of children's self-motivated interaction with the environment and with people around them (see chapter 11). Children learn best by doing, by initiating their own discovery processes, because full participation in group life allows them to fulfill biologically based social and learning needs simultaneously. Not only should children be able to draw a sense of security from the group they are part of, they should also have a sense of their own influence in that group as well. They need to be part of a group that is partly theirs, and learning should be a process through which children discover how to be competent participants.

As noted in the previous chapter, there is no inherent dichotomy between the ancient activities of learning (i.e., observing, imitating, playing, and exploring) and the acquisition of new cognitive skills necessary to survival and well-being in a modern technological environment. The school does not have to be an alienating transition between family life and adult life in a bureaucratic society. In fact, a great deal of evidence indicates that, when children are influential participants in their own learning, they acquire logico-mathematical reasoning skills (so important for success in our culture) more thoroughly and in a more meaningful way than when they are passive recipients of information (Piaget 1973). There is no necessary gap between the processes of social development that satisfy biologically based needs and the processes of intellectual development that prepare children for life in the modern world.

Two brief examples of how this perspective can be used to question old assumptions about the environment of learning in the school might help clarify this important principle. It is often said that *a classroom should be quiet*. No doubt there are certain intellectual activities that may at times be better performed in silence than in a noisy room. But if participation in the learning process is a critical part of a child's social and cognitive development, then the choice to be in a quiet place at a particular time ought to be, at least in part, the child's own. A learning *community*, on the other hand, should probably be full of conversation and activity, play and interaction. We have seen how much talk goes on in foraging societies, and there is no reason to expect that a classroom full of children in a modern society would behave any differently if not suppressed.

A second common assumption is that *students should do their own work*. But why should children do their own work if human learning is social and participatory in nature? There are only two serious reasons for requiring children to do their own work, and both are negative. First, the size of the educational environment prohibits effective participation; second, quantitative evaluations of individual performance are useless for assessing group processes. When children explore together, share notions, challenge one another's perceptions, and work out problems in a group, they do more than learn the material presented to them. They discover and create ways in which that material is meaningful in their lives, and more generally, they learn how to be competent participants in a group.

From an evolutionary perspective there is absolutely no excuse for requiring children to do their own work, unless they want to. One vision of the use of computer technology in the learning process is of individual students working out computer-generated problems, each sitting at his or her own terminal. An alternative vision, informed by an evolutionary perspective, is of groups of three or four children gathered about a terminal taking turns, playing, observing, experimenting, kibitzing, laughing, scuffling, goofing off, showing off, and working out computer-generated problems as a group.

THE DEVELOPMENT OF SKILLS

All skills that children acquire and master are important components of their learning and their identity. An evolutionary perspective helps us see that intellectual skills are only a part of the repertoire a child needs to become a productive, responsible adult and that the structure of formal education must be changed significantly.

A child's formal education should begin with activities that develop manual and mechanical skills that most children can acquire and that allow everyone to participate. Elementary schools should focus on creating opportunities for play and for projects that require children to cooperate and work out solutions to problems as a group.

In the appropriate elementary school young children would work a lot with their hands. They would build and make things. They would also take things apart to explore them. There would be academic instruction in elementary school, but the development of cognitive skills would come as a supplement to collaborative building, making, or play activities—not the other way around, as is currently the case. Through such activities children could form a common base of skill that all share. If they are allowed to work through these activities at least partly on their own, they will also build a clear sense both of the group that is formed by the project workers and of the individual qualities of the group members. Furthermore, if the "survival skills of the Information Age" are presented to children in a larger, more inclusive context, children will have a much clearer notion of how they are used and what they are for than they presently do (see below and chapter 12).

Children need to have some say about the activities they engage in and when they engage in them, and so in the appropriate school a considerable amount of time would be set aside for children themselves to choose what they will do and whom they will do it with. This thought may be frightening for teachers who are used to large groups of children on the one hand and the demands of an established curriculum on the other. But if learning groups are small, if children are allowed to be important participants in the activity, if groups are not always made up of children the same age, and, perhaps most important, if there is a meaningful adult context within which children choose their activities, the children's choice should be both stimulating for them and manageable for the adults involved.

The importance of the self-esteem and self-confidence children can acquire as a result of their being able to choose, at least part of the time, the activities they engage in cannot be overemphasized. And an evolutionary perspective suggests that, if the major context of their choice was shared manual skills rather than unevenly distributed academic skills, the activities chosen would tend to be more inclusive and collaborative.

Another important benefit for children who are able to choose how they will spend their time is that they will be able to discover what they are most drawn to and what they are best at on their own terms rather than on those imposed by adults. In the appropriate school some children may use this time to get out tools and start a building project on their own, while other children may gather around a microcomputer to play games or draw with the computer program Logo. Still others may want to read on their own, others will draw, and others may play music. The point is that, through this selection process, children will begin to understand *for themselves* what kinds of skills come most easily for them and which activities give them the greatest satisfaction. Those who are drawn to making things and working with their hands should have plenty of opportunity, *from the beginning of their formal education*, to explore their abilities and the extent of the attraction. Those who are drawn to cognitive pursuits should have the same opportunity to explore their inclinations.

It might be said that children already have a considerable amount of choice. There are, after all, vocational high schools in which young men and women can learn trade skills rather than focus on academic learning. The problem with trade schools in particular and tracking in general is that the *real* decisions about what children will do and where they will go are made years before high school — by adults, in a narrow context in which academic skills are more highly valued than other kinds of skills. It is no secret in our culture that trade schools are for adolescents who have struggled academically. Vocational education is considered by many to be a kind of consolation prize for those who have had a hard time in junior high school, and the "vokie" stigma reflects educational and cultural values that these children must deal with for a lifetime.

If children's education began with a concentration on so-called vocational skills but also exposed children to a wide range of activities in their communities (see chapter 12) and allowed those drawn by intellectual abstraction to follow their inclinations, the hierarchical valuation of skills in the schools would be broken down. Children would not be constrained to judge their own activities and predispositions by the artificial standard of the culture of education. It is even possible that increased respect for a wide range of skills and abilities would be extended from the school into the society at large.

ADULT MODELS

Children need adult models of behavior that they observe and imitate and that form the core of their understanding of the world. So powerful is the child's need to derive meaning through the behavior of adults that he or she will follow adults into patterns of activity and attitude that make the fulfillment of other crucial needs impossible. The usual structure of public education, especially in the later grades, provides children with pasteboard adults, experts who demand obedience and respect but who rarely demonstrate the competence they supposedly possess in a manner children can use. Thus another principle of the appropriate school is that children must see a variety of adults in a variety of roles. That is, the "teachers" a child encounters in his or her formal education should not all be professional educators.

It is common for people who have been through the public school system in the United States to have had a special teacher, a person who brought literature to life or made history accessible. Perhaps it was a shop teacher who was able to convey pride of skill in craftmanship, or a basketball coach who helped athletes conceive of the whole game in addition to teaching them technical skill. These adults often become models of behavior that deeply affect children's lives. In my case, I became an English major in college solely because of Mrs. Nelson, my senior English teacher in high school.

An evolutionary perspective helps us see what is at work in this powerful interaction between a child and the special teacher. Most important, the special teacher is someone who is deeply and personally engaged in the material being presented to the child. Special teachers are *practitioners* — in history, carpentry, or sports. Mrs. Nelson was a passionate reader of great literature who *demonstrated* the value of writing and ideas to her students. Acknowledgment of the importance of teachers who do what they teach underlies Bruner's belief that "the school must also contain men and women who, in their own way, seek and embody excellence. This does not mean that we shall have to staff our schools with men and women of great genius but that the teacher must embody in his own approach to learning a pursuit of excellence" (1979, 119).

The model of behavior that children receive from the special teacher has meaning because it is something the adult chooses to do and believes is important. Children do not need to be with adults who are trying to think like children or who are trying simply to facilitate the child's learning experience. They need real-life images of what it is like to be an adult who *cares* about something and can demonstrate that concern. What makes Shakespeare irrelevant to children in public schools today is not archaic language, unfamiliar dramatic situations, or characters foreign to American high school students but the fact that, for many high school English teachers, Shakespeare is also irrelevant. These teachers present Shakespeare to children because they must. He *has* to be in the curriculum. But overburdened and underpaid teachers are often unable to describe, much less demonstrate, Shakespeare's importance because they do not actually feel it themselves. They cannot serve as models for children in this regard and instead often communicate their own boredom with the material. The model for children is the adult's *response* to Shakespeare, not what the adult *says* about the bard, much less Shakespeare's plays themselves.

But even a school staffed wholly by special teachers would be an artificial place if the subjects they engaged in were all intellectually based and arranged in a specialized, fragmented, and hierarchical manner. In such a situation the finest special teachers in the world could create at best a kind of "alternate reality" for children — one with emotional depth and meaning, but artificial nonetheless. At this point Dreeben's argument about the transitional nature of the schools (see chapter 9) begins to make sense from an evolutionary perspective.

Children need to see a fuller range of adult activity than they are currently exposed to in the public schools — whether these schools are vocationally or academically oriented. They need to see a range of work, a diversity of attitudes toward the same kind of work, and a variety of skill levels.

In addition to exposure to special teachers and to a range of activities in which adults are purposefully engaged, children need to see individual adults in a variety of roles. In small communities children may sometimes know teachers in less formal capacities — as fellow churchmembers, for example, or as neighbors. An evolutionary perspective suggests that this kind of extracurricular interaction between the adult who is the teacher and the schoolchild helps the child get a clearer view of the adult world. If Ms. Jones, the history teacher, also acts in a community theater group, she exists for many children in two dimensions simultaneously. She is a person, someone who has personal interests, skills, and gifts. She contributes to the accuracy of a schoolchild's version of adult reality. In larger communities and when teachers do not live in the communities they teach in, these outside connections become less and less probable. But if the schools were in better touch with the communities in which they are located and if community members were more sensitive to the needs of children for a range of adult models, a legitimate adult context for children's learning might be built from a cooperation between education professionals and community members (see chapter 12).

OTHER CHILDREN

The strict age-grade segregation that exists in most public schools today is also detrimental to a child's preparation for adult life. Younger children learn a great deal from older children, and older children learn from younger children what they need to know in order to become effective parents. In the appropriate school there would be ample time for children of different age-groups to be together. For example, if a group of fifth- and six-graders elect to build a model of a house during their free time, a group of younger children should be able to observe, ask questions, and participate as far as they are able. Younger children ought to be able to watch older children working with a computer, and older children (not always adults) should be in a position to help the young figure out how the machine works and what can be done with it.

A high school could not be responsible, say, for supplying infants for teenagers to observe and learn from. It is possible, however, for high school students to spend some of their time working in day-care centers or doing repairs or renovations for preschools or teaching in elementary schools in their home communities (see chapter 12).

THE ELDERLY

In the same manner, children need to learn about age from the aged, for the perception of continuity in living—the knowledge that they will some-day be old—should affect choices children make as they prepare for adulthood and thus the choices they make as adults. Knowing about old age and death need not make children "grow up faster," in the way this phrase is used today. But this knowledge can give them a more accurate view of adult life to invoke when they do finally "acquire their intelligence." The cult of youth would not have been possible without first shutting away the elderly. We hide the old folks and refuse to think about our own inexorable aging. Then when we ourselves become old we complain about how we are treated. An evolutionarily appropriate school would include the elderly, would seek them out and design activities in which they would spend time with children (see chapter 12), would demonstrate what they know, and would talk among themselves with children present.

These principles of the evolutionarily appropriate school are, to be sure, roughly sketched here, but they can be useful in planning and evaluating educational programs. Most important, they can be applied on any level of children's learning, from parent deliberations at home to school-board budget deliberations. Individual teachers may apply an evolutionary per-spective in the management of their classes or in the way they communi-cate with school administrators, other teachers, and parents. Parents may be less intimidated by education professionals if they consider how far children's learning ranges, and teachers and school administrators may demand greater community involvement in the school if they acknowl-edge the connection between learning and social competence.

11

An Evolutionary Perspective and
Issues in Educational Philosophy

MANY of the leading educational theorists of the twentieth century have found pieces of the picture of children's learning that emerges from a study of evolution, for observation of what children respond to most enthusiastically will lead one to most if not all of the principles presented in the last chapter. An evolutionary view, however, gives us the ability to locate our observations in a truly panhuman context, a framework within which we can examine wishful ideology and immediate reactions to social and historical problems.

In this chapter I review some important issues in educational philosophy to see how the work of several influential thinkers fits into the paradigm that has been developed in this book. I have made no attempt to provide a comprehensive overview of educational thought in this chapter, nor have I presented every existing perspective on the issues discussed. My goal here is to offer brief examples, using generally accepted problems in education and classic texts, of how an evolutionary perspective may inform educational thought.

HOW CHILDREN LEARN BEST

Piaget's observations led him to the conclusion that a child, like any living organism, *seeks* interaction with its environment. According to Piaget, children possess innate tendencies, or "functional invariants," common to all animals. Children act to *organize* their experience, and they *adapt* in an environment through processes Piaget termed *assimilation* and *accommodation*. Assimilation is the incorporation of aspects of the environment into the child's organizational system, while accommodation involves a modification of the child's organizational system in response to the environment. *Equilibration* is Piaget's term for the effort to attain a balance between these two processes of adaptation. For Piaget, cognitive development in children is an interaction between the autoregulatory processes of the child (including physical maturation, the tendency to organize, and the tendency to adapt) and the environment (including, of course, the social environment) in which the child lives.

The implication of this interactionist view of intellectual development for formal education is that

> the development of intelligence, as it emerges from the recent research . . . is dependent upon natural, or spontaneous, processes, in the sense that they may be utilized and accelerated by education at home or in school but that they are not derived from that education and, on the contrary, constitute the preliminary and necessary condition of efficacity in any form of instruction. (Piaget 1971, 36)

The organic equilibration processes of the child *require* interaction with the environment, according to Piaget, and the activities of play, imitation, and investigation are integral elements of these processes. Piaget also insists that social interaction, conversation, argument, and so forth are extremely important modes of learning, for, among other things, they set up *disequilibria* that the child acts to reconcile. This reconciliation results in new learning and helps move the child from one stage of development to the next. Thus, according to Piaget, children need to work things through together as they encounter and learn to solve problems (see Ginsburg and Opper 1969).

Another important implication of Piaget's work for education is that the child must be a full participant in the learning process. Since children in various stages of development are quite different from adults (Piaget 1971), it follows that they must be able to deploy their attention and make their investigations as much as possible in their own way. Adults cannot experience what a child experiences or think the way a child thinks, so learning environments or processes that are set up for children entirely by adults are likely to exclude something vital to the learning child.

Piaget emphasizes that, although children may be taught to make certain responses to particular stimuli, as the behaviorists have noted, there is no true understanding unless children are at the stage at which such understanding is possible and they "invent" the principles that characterize each stage in their own way (Piaget 1973, 93). For Piaget, all children's learning, including the development of logico-mathematical reasoning, is best done in environments that allow the child plenty of room to experiment and explore.

In the latter part of his life, Piaget wrestled with the problem of how the processes of evolution were revealed in a child's cognitive development (1971, 1976, 1980). But his evolutionary perspective focuses almost exclusively on intellectual development, seen as the *structure* of behavior, while emotional systems are seen as rather vague forces that energize cognitive development.

> All the authors agree that in all behavior the structure is cognitive, and the force, or the economy, is affective. Therefore, affect cannot be the cause of a cognitive structure, any more than intelligence can be the cause of affect, because a structure is not the cause of this energy, this force and vice versa. Between the two is a relation of correspondence, and not of causality. (Quoted in Modgil 1974, 369)

In terms of the emotional systems described in this book, the question of causality in the relationship between emotional systems and cognitive systems is beside the point. The young primate is motivated to seek contact with its environment and engage in the kinds of equilibrium-producing processes Piaget describes by emotional systems that mediate not only the direct activities of learning but the entire environment in which learning takes place.

Piaget's work is of inestimable value for the understanding of children's cognitive development. But his preference for the intellect—and particularly his proposition that Western, logico-mathematical reasoning is the highest state of human intellectual development — has contributed to the split between cognition and emotion. Piaget's (and others') preference for intellectual processes leads one to believe that the cognitive is more significant than the emotional, and the assumption that cognitive and emotional systems are linked only by so-called correspondences makes the split seem less critical than it is.

Piaget's thought lends authority to the separation of children into age-groups during their educational experiences. If children in a particular stage are *incapable* of understanding certain concepts or performing certain kinds of operations, it follows that in school they should be grouped together in terms of the stages of their development. Such a grouping would minimize the chances of presenting a world to children that is incomprehensible to some and boring to others.

Surely if our sole intent in the education of children is to develop their intellectual abilities as efficiently as possible, it makes sense to segregate them on the basis of age. If we take into consideration a wider range of human activity, however, it may be seen that school environments structured to facilitate only intellectual development may actually inhibit the development of other significant areas of life. If, for example, children need to learn about childhood and childrearing by being with other children of different ages and stages, we are making a mistake when we make them spend *all* their school time in age-mate (or even "stage-mate") groups.

Jerome Bruner also emphasizes the importance of personal discovery in children's learning but falls into the same cognitive trap that Piaget does. Both arrive at similar conclusions concerning the activities of learning and the role of the child as learner. Bruner, like Piaget, rejects mechanistic behaviorism and argues that understanding for a child must come as an "act of discovery" (1979). The child must have a certain amount of control over his or her own learning process, must interact with the material to be learned, and must manipulate it in his or her own way. In this manner, according to Bruner, children are able to establish a system of *intrinsic* rewards in place of the *extrinsic* rewards that traditionally characterize children's education. "The hypothesis I would propose here is that to the degree that one is able to approach learning as a task of discovering something rather than "learning about" it, to that degree there will be a tendency for the child to work with the autonomy of self-reward or, more properly, to be rewarded by discovery itself" (1979, 88).

The "intrinsic rewards" Bruner refers to are surely associated with the emotional systems I have described in this book, but Bruner, like Piaget, does not devote much space to emotional systems. For Bruner a school should be an environment in which the activities of the intellect can become their own reward. Schools should provide "more than a continuity with the broader community or with everyday experience. It is primarily the special community where one experiences discovery by the use of intelligence, where one leaps into new and unimagined realms of experience, experience that is discontinuous with what went before" (1979, 118).

But for most of human history intellectual achievement, like other forms of achievement, took place in a full-scale, continuous social environment. It is impossible to avoid the impact of social emotions in the movement from extrinsic to intrinsic rewards that Bruner has observed in the learning process. If children are interested in the "growth and maintenance of mastery" (Bruner 1979, 92) for the intrinsic rewards that accompany this acquisition, is it not likely that the perception and acknowledgment of this mastery by others — adults and peers — is a significant component of the reward? From this perspective one might offer the same criticism of Bruner as of Piaget: If intellectual achievement is the major criterion of importance or status in the school, a good many children will never have the opportunity of experiencing the intrinsic rewards of intellectual investigation. They will be blocked by the very emphasis on mind work in school if they are unable to become competent at a time and in a manner the school demands.

John Dewey, on the other hand, was well aware of the problems associated with abstraction in education. In order to avoid the alienation of a school that focused on abstract operations and the acquisition of disconnected information, he proposed that the child's personal experience serve as the starting place for formal education. Like Piaget and Bruner, Dewey concentrated on the importance of the development of the individual and insisted that children must have a significant role in what and how they learn. The methods of education that follow from these assumptions are first that the pupil have a genuine situation of experience — that there be a continuous activity in which he is interested for its own sake; secondly, that a genuine problem develop within this situation as a stimulus to thought; third, that he possess the information and make the observations needed to deal with it; fourth, that suggested solutions occur to him which he shall be responsible for developing in an orderly way; fifth, that he have opportunity and occasion to test his ideas by application, to make their meaning clear and to discover for himself their validity. (Dewey [1916] 1961, 192)

Once again, the emphasis is on discovery, on interaction with the environment. But Dewey also laid a great deal of emphasis on the *social* relations that such interaction generates. Dewey's focus was both on individual intellectual development and on education-as-socialization, and thus for Dewey, the purposes of formal education were more inclusive than they were for either Piaget or Bruner. Through the process of education children should be able to realize their full individual potential, should be able to acquire skills necessary to adapt successfully to a changing environment, and should become responsible citizens in a democracy.

One implication of concentrating on the real-life experiences of individuals in formal education is that the school assumes a far more powerful socializing role. When part of the *content* of education is a child's personal experience, then values, beliefs, and prejudices come to the surface. The learning-group members become participants in one another's lives, and the teacher becomes more like a parent. But Dewey was interested in building a coherent society in addition to developing individual minds. The education of the young was an opportunity to create a social order that would be democratic and participatory because it was founded upon the "freedom of intelligence, that is to say, freedom of observation and of judgment exercised in behalf of purposes that are intrinsically worthwhile" ([1938] 1963, 61). According to Dewey, if members of a society have this freedom and learn the skills of organizing and interpreting their experiences, a coherence and balance will emerge in the society, and the clear relationship between individual achievement and social good will become obvious.

Where we now see only the outward doing and the outward product, there, behind all visible results, is the readjustment of mental attitude, the enlarged and sympathetic vision, the sense of growing power, and the willing ability to identify both insight and capacity with the interest of the world and man. Unless culture be a superficial polish, a veneering of mahogany over common wood, it surely is this—the growth of the imagination in flexibility, in scope, and sympathy, till the life which the individual lives is informed with the life of nature and of society. (1956, 61–62)

In Dewey's philosophy, an individual child's sense of growing power and mastery could best take place in an "organization in which all individuals have an opportunity to contribute something" ([1938] 1963, 56), and he thus viewed the school as a society in which children should be full participants and in which all would have status because the criteria for achievement would be determined by the group itself in the context of the real-life experiences of group members. "Social control" in such a group would be a natural by-product of the give-and-take among peers. Dewey saw that not only was individual learning facilitated in such democratic groups but children who learned in these environments acquired a deeper understanding of others in the process.

John Dewey probably never knew how close his theories came to describing the processes of learning in primate and nomadic foraging societies. His work can be viewed as an attempt to reconstruct the balances that are part of the human adaptation and have been lost. His attributing the integration of personal development and social responsibility to *culture* is, however, upside down, for the desire to have the integration *underlies* every culture. What is the social control Dewey refers to if not the establishment of balance between the desire to belong to the group and the need to stand out as an individual?

THE ADULT ROLE IN CHILDREN'S LEARNING

Dewey understood that the "greater maturity of the teacher" should "arrange conditions" for learning ([1938], 1963, 47) and envisioned an almost reciprocal arrangement between teacher and students. The student explores and the teacher proposes experiments in an effort to find the best learning process for each individual student. Both teacher and student are thus challenged, but the teacher, as an adult, has greater responsibility.

> The educator is responsible for a knowledge of individuals and for a knowledge of subject-matter that will enable activities to be selected which lend themselves to social organization, an organization in which all individuals have an opportunity to contribute something and in which the activities in which all participate are the chief carrier of control. ([1938] 1963, 56)

Unfortunately, John Dewey did not realize how important it was for teachers to be *practicing adults* who demonstrate adult reality to children. As a result, a range of alternative models of education have arisen since Dewey's time that have gone several steps beyond Dewey's recommended balance between the adult teacher's guidance and the child's freedom to explore. In such alternatives children "learn independently, not in bunches. . . . They learn out of interest and curiosity, not to please or appease the adults in power; and . . . they ought to be in control of their own learning, deciding for themselves what they want to learn and how they want to learn it" (Holt 1967, 169).

This concept of children's learning led to the creation of the English alternative school Summerhill, by A. S. Neill (1960). Neill, Holt, and others who expanded the progressive tradition were trying to establish an emotional reality — a community — that could *compensate* for the negative experiences children have had or may have in the world at large. As John Holt says in support of the Summerhill model:

> Over the years, many children have gone to Summerhill who were wholly defeated and demoralized by life, locked in their desperate protective strategies of self-defense and deliberate failure, filled with fear, suspicion, anger, and hatred. . . . Most of the children there get well. They get back their strength, confidence, and courage, and turn to face life and to move out into it, as all healthy children really want to do. (1970, 85)

And Neill himself writes: "Summerhill is possibly the happiest school in the world. We have no truants and seldom a case of homesickness. We very rarely have fights. . . . I seldom hear a child cry, because children when free have much less hate to express than children who are downtrodden (1960, 8).

Summerhill and similar schools have been criticized on various grounds, including their isolation from the realities of life and what Paul Goodman calls a "latitudinarian lack of standards" (1970, 215). But there is a more serious problem. There is, in these alternatives, little or no direction from adults.

We have seen that, in both primate and nomadic foraging societies, youngsters grow and learn in a framework of intimate relationships between subsistence and sociality. In these societies "direction from adults" is in everything a child sees and does, for the framework itself is the guide for all. Children *must* have adult models, and the point is that they *do* have them whether or not the adults like it or accept responsibility for serving as these models.

The problem with Summerhill is not so much that children are being socialized for environments that do not really exist in the world outside the alternative school. They are being presented with adult models of behavior that do not prepare them for any adult reality. When the adults on whom children must model their behavior are engaged only in smoothing the way for children, children cannot gain a vision of what they should become.

THE SCHOOL AND THE CULTURE AT LARGE

Should the schools teach traditional cultural values? Or should they be agents of social reform? Do the schools provide opportunity for children from disadvantaged groups, or do they condition children to accept their lot in a hierarchical society? These conflicting concepts of the function of schools can be resolved — at least to a certain extent — in the framework of the evolutionary perspective. Before identifying the principles that can bring these views together, I briefly review two classically antagonistic positions in education.

In *The Higher Learning in America* (1936), R. M. Hutchins described an idealized education in which the best elements of the past informed the present and helped stabilize the future. For Hutchins, institutions of formal learning in the United States should preserve, elucidate, and pass on the highest achievements and the finest artifacts of the culture. Understanding the past should provide the young with a framework for making decisions in the present and planning for the future. A general education program should thus be "a course of study consisting of the greatest books of the western world and the arts of reading, writing, thinking, and speaking, together with mathematics, the best exemplar of the processes of human reason" (p. 85). These truths of Western culture are, for Hutchins, a legacy, a sacred trust that must be transmitted from master to student with the utmost integrity.

There is a wistful regret in *The Higher Learning*, a longing for former times. "Those happy days are gone forever," Hutchins laments in reference to the Middle Ages — a time when European universities were havens where students could seek the truth (p. 43). It is enlightening to read the most recent edition (1961) of *The Higher Learning*, for in it Hutchins includes a preface that acknowledges the profundity of the changes that took place in United States society between 1936 and 1961. Hutchins is distressed by such changes, for they represent to him a disintegration of the social order, a fragmentation and trivialization of meaning. What fragmentation and triviality might he find in the late 1980s?

One of the clearly articulated assumptions of *The Higher Learning* is that any society must have a foundation that is common to all its members or it will fall apart. That base, for Hutchins, was the classical Western tradition, and he believed that a comprehensive educational program that taught young people the skills of thought and expression in this context would provide the foundation for a "rational social order" (p. xix). Certainly today's "back to basics" movement in public schools across the country is in this same tradition, and from this perspective it is not surprising that, in its 1983 report, *A Nation at Risk*, the National Commission on Excellence in Education recommended

> that State and local high school graduation requirements be strengthened and that, at a minimum, all students seeking a diploma be required to lay the foundations in the Five New Basics by taking the following curriculum during their 4 years of high school: (a) 4 years of English; (b) 3 years of mathematics; (c) 3 years of science;

(d) 3 years of social studies; and (e) one-half year of computer science. For the college-bound, 2 years of foreign language in high school are strongly recommended in addition to those taken earlier. (P. 24)

In recent years several radical critiques of the schools and their functions have been developed from the opposite point of view. These critiques chastise the schools for perpetuating the cultural values of a society that is at best mistaken and at worst unjust. Raymond Callahan's classic study *Education and the Cult of Efficiency* (1962) describes the development of standardization, large size, routinization, and so forth in American education in terms of the nation's wholesale adoption of business methods and modes of evaluation in the first thirty years of this century. The ways in which teachers were paid, school systems funded, books chosen, materials purchased, and children instructed—all were casualties of an attempt to "hedge the bet" with children's education; that is, to obtain the most for the least.

The tragedy itself was fourfold: that educational questions were subordinated to business considerations; that administrators were produced who were not, in any true sense, educators; that a scientific label was put on some very unscientific and dubious methods and practices; and that an anti-intellectual climate, already prevalent, was strengthened. As the business-industrial values and procedures spread into the thinking and acting of educators, countless educational decisions were made on economic or on non-educational grounds. (Pp. 246–47)

Callahan believed that education in the United States had fallen into an unlucky historical trap, but in the past twenty years new critics of formal education insist that the incorporation of business methods and models into the educational system in this country was no accident. From one perspective at least, they say, the schools are working very well indeed. Because these authors urge a revision of old notions about the achievements and opportunities of formal schooling in the United States, they have been called Revisionists (see e.g., Spring 1976; Katz 1975; Bowles and Gintis 1976; Illich 1970; Kozol 1975).

According to the Revisionists, the schools are socializing children into specific, limited roles that are designed to perpetuate their powerlessness and ensure their complicity in maintaining the status quo. The schools are "sorting machines" (Spring 1976) that separate the elite of the society from those who are to do the society's menial tasks. But even the elite absorb through their schooling attitudes and behavior that will contribute not at all to their individual fulfillment but that are essential to the smooth running of the capitalist enterprise (Bowles and Gintis 1976). The Revisionists argue that the society itself, dominated and controlled as it is by a power elite, can simply not tolerate the kind of intellectual development Piaget and Bruner advocate or the kind of school/community Dewey dreamed of. According to Bowles and Gintis in their aptly entitled article "If John Dewey Calls . . . Tell Him Things Didn't Work Out," "The way in which the school system helps to produce a stratified and alienated labor force for the capitalist enterprise is inconsistent with its serving to further individual self-development or equality of opportunity" (1974, 8).

These critiques are serious indictments of the culture itself, as it is revealed through an examination of one of its most important institutions, formal education. From the Revisionist perspective, Hutchins is guilty of, at best, well-meaning cultual imperialism, and Dewey is merely naive. If the culture itself is unacceptable, nothing short of massive social change will do. Jonathan Kozol put this idea pretty clearly in 1975: "Schools cannot at once both socialize to the values of an oppressor and toil for the liberation and the potency of the oppressed. If innovation is profound, it is subversive. If it is subversive, it is incompatible with the prime responsibilities of the public school" (p. 211). And a year later Bowles and Gintis issued a similar challenge: "People must choose, and choose to fight for, socialism as a positive alternative based on a serious, desirable, and feasible vision. This vision must develop in the course of struggle, but the struggle will not develop without it" (1976, 286).

For many years educational thinkers who believed a reform of society was necessary identified institutions of formal education as potential agents of this social reform. This grand purpose for formal education suffuses the work of Dewey, as we have seen, and it is also present in Hutchins, who writes that "upon education our country must pin its hopes of true progress" (1936, 119). The most optimistic school reformer in this vein was Theodore Brameld, who challenged public school instructors to become "teacher citizens with convictions" who are not afraid to "exhibit these in the public square" (1956, 338).

But the Revisionist critique does not call for reform in the schools as a way of solving social problems. Indeed, the Revisionists have concluded that reform of public schooling is impossible, given the fact that schools are cultural institutions. In addition, in recent years convincing arguments have been made that, simply because the schools *are* institutions and complex organizations, they have their own reality—their own internal structure and logic. For this reason alone, they will resist reform, just as institutions in any society resist reform (see Hurn 1985). As Hurn maintains, the schools are probably neither as evil as the Revisionists claim nor as beneficent as educational liberals have claimed in the past, but they are surely bureaucracies that will act to protect themselves and avoid significant change.

This bureaucratic aspect of public education is a tremendous obstacle to reform. Children must be "prepared" for junior high school in the fifth and sixth grades so that they will not have too traumatic a transition from elementary school. Thus even the most enlightened elementary school teachers find themselves in a double bind. If they hold true to beliefs about, say, the negative effects of grading or the damage done to learning by fragmenting and abstracting the curriculum, they run the risk of delivering unsuspecting children into an alien and terrifying environment. In the same way, teachers and administrators are constrained to present a united front to school boards and parents, despite deep disagreements about educational practice and philosophy that may exist among them. The system feeds upon itself and provides concrete reasons for doing things in ways that make absolutely no sense except within the system.

The Revisionists are more radical than some in their call for social revolution, but it is important to note that most studies of formal education, regardless of the ideological persuasion of the author, share an assumption that the society is the school's biggest problem. The society that fosters such bureaucracy and perpetuates absurdities and inequalities must be reformed. Upon this point, if no other, Hutchins, Dewey, and Jonathan Kozol are agreed.

An evolutionary perspective, too, leads one to a conviction that contemporary societies are flawed and that schools are no better than the cultures they serve. Ours is a society in which a great many people exist but too few belong, a society in which too few people are recognized as individuals. In our culture people's experiences are so diversified that only abstractions can serve to link them to one another. Above all, ours is a society in which children must wait in the wings until they are pushed out onto the stage of adult life with a jumble of lines from a hundred different plays and no idea of who they are supposed to be.

As a species, we are adapted to social structures in which the need to belong is intertwined with and balanced by the equally deep need for personal identity and status in the group. Male or female, young or old, all need to belong and at the same time to be individually important. When these needs are not fulfilled in the context of each other, humans suffer (and often make other humans suffer).

Human learning evolved as a way of preparing for and becoming competent in this dynamic balance, and the activities of learning that characterize the species are perfectly appropriate to this ancient purpose. Small wonder that, in a society that is separated from the physical environment, that regularly separates individual importance and group attachment and intellect and emotion—a society in which the adults themselves are not sure what adulthood is supposed to be—institutions of formal education also demonstrate these separations and perpetuate them in children.

The study of the evolutionary antecedents of children's learning leads us to two conclusions that can shed light on this difficult debate between those who would teach the culture in the schools and those who would reform the culture altogether. First, it is not enough to teach the lore and values of a particular culture or a particular ideology in the schools. Studying the great books of Western society will not produce the kind of social stability Hutchins longed for, nor will studying Marx produce the utopian socialism dreamed by Bowles and Gintis, because both are being offered in learning environments that are bureaucratized, over-specialized, and isolated from other social environments. Furthermore, human beings are not adapted for cultures or for ideologies but for relationships, interactions, and learning processes. Surely children must know about the culture they belong to and must acquire the skills that allow them to flourish in that culture. The culture itself, however, demands behavior and attitudes that reduce children's chances of establishing social balances that satisfy ancient emotional needs, and we do the young (and ourselves) a great disservice if we simply insist that they follow in erring footsteps.

Second, the schools (and the society, if we ever get that far) must be reformed along lines that take into consideration the biologically based emotional systems that underlie the human learning adaptation. In addition, it is important to include in the curriculum of formal education the idea that we are tied to one another as human beings and to other forms of life on earth through the processes of evolution. With such reforms accomplished, the schools may very well become agents of social change.

How may these reforms be accomplished? Is it really possible that modifications can be made in the schools that will have a positive impact on the larger society? In the next chapter I examine the environments of a couple of possible schools in some detail so as to identify particular problems that need to be addressed. But before considering such schools, it seems fitting to close this chapter with a brief discussion of a fourth important issue in educational thought.

HUMAN NATURE

As mentioned in the Introduction, one of the most troublesome misunderstandings in educational thought results from dual, even contradictory, assumptions people make about "human nature." On the one hand, many theories imply that there are specifically human ways of being, human capacities, and human modes of learning. On the other hand some maintain that humans are not constrained by this humanness in any significant way. As noted in the Introduction, Coleman and Erikson both apparently had ideas about what was natural in the socialization of adolescents. Their recommendations for change, however, were offered in terms of historical, rather recent adolescent experience. Hutchins contends that "one purpose of education is to draw out the elements of our common human nature. These elements are the same in any time or place" (1936, 66). Yet, as we have seen, he also exhorts us to create a "rationally ordered society" that is not necessarily founded on our shared understanding of the common elements of our nature. Bowles and Gintis urge "the development and articulation of the vision of a socialist alternative"

(1976, 288) which, as noted above, "people must choose, and choose to fight for" (p. 286). At the same time, they assert that "the social and economic conditions of socialism will facilitate the full development of human capacities. These capacities are for cooperative, democratic, equal, and participatory human relationships; for cultural, emotional, and sensual fulfillment" (p. 266).

There is the sense in much educational writing that all we have to do is try harder to put our intellectual visions of a free and well-ordered society into operation and we will be able to get the job done. But where did these "human capacities" come from? And if they are indeed panhuman characteristics, are they not more than vague *possibilities* open to essentially unrestrained human beings? Because they developed in the course of human evolution, these capacities exert pressure on our behavior in any environment. And like other biologically based capacities, they have their limits.

The confusion that exists in educational thought between the human ability to adapt and what humans do naturally is certainly related to the gap that has developed in human life between intellectual and emotional systems. For a long time our focus has been on the development of cognitive systems and as noted above, when one's measurement of achievement is confined to this particular area of human activity, it appears that there is no limit to what we humans can do. Indeed, perhaps in the purely intellectual sense, there is no limit (if the species survives). But if we include social behavior and emotional need in our definitions of capacity, our adaptability breaks down. An evolutionary perspective indicates that our hopes for the future and our ideas of what humans can achieve socially must be made less abstract, brought down to earth and into the group. In other words, if we must re-create human society, let us attempt to do so with as clear an understanding as possible of the biological needs that are our evolutionary heritage. Otherwise, we will always be working, in some capacity, against ourselves.

12

The Possible School:
Work Experience Classroom
and Ring Day Care Center

IN this chapter I offer two examples of how an evolutionary perspective can provide a theoretical base for educational programs that address children's social and emotional needs. The first example is derived from my personal experience as the director of and a teacher in an urban alternative school for adolescents and adults. The second is a brief description of a day-care center for preschool children. My goal in this chapter is to suggest the range an evolutionary perspective can have in education and to show how this framework for understanding children's learning may knit together the perceptions of educators working with children of different ages in different settings.

WORK EXPERIENCE CLASSROOM

For four and a half years, from 1975 to 1979, I was involved in alternative education for high school dropouts—both adolescents and adults. The program was funded by the Comprehensive Employment Training Act (CETA) as part of Work Experience Programs and grew from one-on-one tutoring of a handful of teenagers to a school that was fully integrated with the job-training and counseling activities of Work Experience Programs and was part of a referral network that included six different school districts. Between 1976 and April, 1979, a total of 176 students who had studied in Work Experience Classroom obtained a General Educational

Development (GED, or high school equivalency) certificate, and by 1978 more than 130 students spent some time each week in the school while also working on training crews (carpentry, auto mechanics, landscaping, and forestry) or in public-service jobs.

It has always been difficult for me to write about Work Experience Classroom. What began as a job became a crusade, so my memories of the school are flooded with emotion. And as I mentioned in the Introduction, we virtually stumbled into whatever successes we had. Yet I have known all along that the very depth of the emotional response staff and students had to Work Experience Classroom was an important key to the program's success, and the stumbling itself was in some part the result of taking seriously the students' responses to what we offered. The quantitative data—how many and what percentage of Work Experience Classroom students raised their reading levels significantly, obtained GED certificates, went on to college, are earning a given salary today, are still holding jobs, are still out of jail—are not adequate to evaluate the learning that took place in this program.

At the same time, it is clear that I am unable to be objective. Before I acquired an evolutionary perspective, the harder I tried to describe the all-important emotional dimensions of the school, the more muddled the description became. My difficulty illustrates the major problem with the qualitative evaluations mentioned in chapter 10. How does one measure "the extent to which children have an understanding of the ways of groups they are part of"—an emotion-charged quality—without utterly losing one's perspective?

In fact, methods of evaluating such qualities in individuals (e.g., Klemp 1977) and the extent to which these qualities are fostered by organizations and institutions (e.g., Firth and Reed 1982) are being developed and tested in education now. Future studies using an evolutionary framework will be able to make these qualitative assessments and then compare them with quantitative data.

An evolutionary perspective has given me new categories in which to place both the affect and the activity of Work Experience Classroom. I briefly describe the ways in which the program either addressed or did not address the principles identified in chapter 10.

Size Although more than 130 students, adults and adolescents, came into Work Experience Classroom during the week, there were never more than thirty-five people in the school at a time. The ratio of students to teachers was about eight to one, so the learning groups that developed in the school were always small. We generally did not divide the students into classes, each having its own teacher. For the most part the learning groups in the school were flexible and formed spontaneously. Teachers and students would sit together at a long table in the main room while in other rooms students read individually or worked in smaller groups.

The central table, in fact, became one of the most important features of the school. Everyone began the day around the table. The crews met at the school before going out on a job, so the crew supervisors, teachers, students, nonstudents, and employment counselors would have coffee together before getting on with the day's work. After the crews left for a job and schoolwork began, the central table became the main study area. On a typical day perhaps twelve students and two or three teachers would be clustered about the table. Some of the students would be working on math, some on English grammar, and some on reading. At one end of the table a question might come up, and a conversation would begin. The conversation might be confined to a student and a teacher, or it might expand to one corner of the table. Sometimes the discussion would be so compelling that the entire table would get involved. Then, eventually, teachers would lead students back to individual or small-group study. The spontaneity of this learning environment and the relative ease with which it was "managed" by the teachers were possible only as long as the group remained small.

Most of the adolescents in the school were part of work crews that consisted of a supervisor and from ten to twelve teenagers. The people in these crews often became very close to one another as they worked through projects and problems. Young people acquired trade skills on these crews, but they also learned how to cooperate with others and how to give and gain respect.

Because these crews were small they could accommodate a tremendous amount of diversity. Black, white, and Puerto Rican youngsters, who avoided each other in the high schools and lived in different neighborhoods or even different towns, were constrained by the size of the group and the nature of the work to see one another as individuals. The same kind of individualization occurred in the school. In the four and a half years I was with Work Experience Classroom, we had only one, brief fight in school.

The kind of learning that people did on the crews or in the school was not possible in a large group. In 1978 the CETA program doubled the number of participants in the school and on the crews without increasing the size of the staff, and the size of the learning groups grew dramatically. Immediately the negative effects of unwieldy size became manifest. Teachers and crew supervisors were forced to create greater structure and regimentation in the program, and *management* became a primary issue. Teachers could spend less time with individual students, and the spontaneity of the central table gradually gave way, first to chaos, then to more rigid rules of behavior. Most important, the scheduling necessary to manage such numbers of workers and students destroyed one of the most significant characteristics of Work Experience Classroom: the opportunity for participants to *choose* whether they would attend the school or not. Precipitously increased size was not the only change that led to the school's demise, but a smaller group might have been able to solve other problems. For a large group the task was impossible.

Power and Participation of Children   In early 1975, the educational component of Work Experience Programs consisted of two teachers, one in Fitchburg and one in Gardner, a smaller city to the west, in which the CETA Consortium office was located. The main activity of the Work Experience branch of the Gardner CETA was job training, and we teachers had been hired to provide the optional maximum of ten hours per week of academic instruction made available to participants. Work Experience Program participants actively had to *choose* academic instruction as part of their program, and the students' voluntary participation in the school empowered them in ways no one could have predicted at the time.

At first the teachers worked with a handful of adolescents who thought that going to school a few hours a week would be easier than being at a job the whole time. (The students were paid at the same job-training hourly rate when in school.) Occasionally an adult in the Adult Career Training or the Senior Training Employment programs would be steered our way. But the demands for more academic education and the chance to obtain a high school equivalency certificate were greater than anyone expected. Within a year the number of Work Experience participants who requested academic instruction had grown to the extent that additional teachers had to be hired in Fitchburg. The "school" that evolved out of this demand for education thus began as an essentially voluntary commitment. Crew workers could decide for themselves whether they would go to the school or not and had a voice in the amount of time they would spend there each week. We saw early on that the *decision* to go to the school was important to a student's success there and tried to maintain the choice for Work Experience participants.

Problems in the school and in the crews were discussed in open meetings in which participants were encouraged to say what they thought and could see that they had an effect on decisions that were made. If these meetings were empowering for all, they were also sometimes a bit daunting for the adults involved. In order to empower the students in the school, we had to give up some of our official power as teachers, supervisors, and administrators. We had to earn the participants' respect as individuals and sometimes had to reexamine our own assumptions, not only about education, but about life in general as well.

Another way in which the students obtained personal power in the school and were, at the same time, drawn to the school community was through the crew work on the school buildings. All four locations the school occupied between 1975 and 1979 were renovated by the crews, and so in a significant way the school belonged to the students. The students were also responsible for maintaining it and keeping it clean (which, unfortunately, meant that it was usually messy—a fact we chose to live with, even though we could have hired a janitor).

Students of all ages had a say in which areas of instruction they would encounter when. The areas of the GED exams (grammar and usage, literature, social studies, natural science, and math) provided a framework of subject areas every student who wanted a high school equivalency had to address. Nevertheless, the periods of time students spent working in these areas, the order in which they engaged them, and the modes through which they were engaged were determined through discussion and negotiation.

As enjoyable as working at the central table was, students were continually faced with the choice of concentrating more pointedly on reading by working alone or extending the time it would take for their reading to improve by working at the table. Teachers made observations and suggestions to students about how they might best make progress, but the ultimate decision was a collaboration. Between 1976 and 1979, only a few students made no progress and were eventually asked to leave the school to make room for those who had more interest in academic learning.

One unplanned result of empowering the students in these ways was that it became important for teachers and crew supervisors to make a case for particular subjects and demonstrate their value as well as teach them. Learning became a dialogue when the students realized that they had some say. When all questions were possible, teachers had to be either competent adults or recognized as incompetent by the students. In a sense, then, the adolescents of Work Experience Classroom also became agents of social control, like children in a foraging society—a role very few were able to play in other parts of their lives. So much had been imposed upon these children from their earliest years that it was difficult for them to believe that they actually did have some power in the school or on the crews. Many, however, went beyond simply using the power they had (as in catching teachers out or making fun of slower learners) and began to take some responsibility for it by asking thoughtful questions and helping others.

I can characterize Work Experience Classroom by referring to the two examples of traditional educational practice critiqued in chapter 10. *A classroom should be quiet*: In general, the alternative school was not a quiet learning environment. Quiet areas were available for those doing work that required silence, but there was usually a lot of chatter, jokes, and laughter around the central table. The conversation in the school served the same purposes it serves in all human societies: it tied people to one another, gave individuals the opportunity to speak up and take center stage, and offered the chance for spontaneous stories in which all could participate. Through the talk in the school or on a job with the crews, young people determined their relationships to one another and to the adults in the community of Work Experience Programs. Some established new identities in the group through their verbal wit and insight. Others listened, preferring to demonstrate their abilities in other ways.

Students should do their own work Although there were many occasions when students did their own work in the school—reading and writing and doing math—much of the education that took place was communal. We awarded no grades, and there was therefore no reason for students to cheat on the tests. The students themselves eventually came to the realization that only skill and knowledge would see them through. They could not "psych out" the system or any of the individual teachers, because we evaluated their performance as workers, students, and community members in the whole program. And these evaluations were made through observation and conversation on the job and in school rather than through tests. The tests we did give students were either initial placement tests or practice tests in preparation for the high school equivalency exam. It was an important feature of Work Experience Classroom that these pretests were used for reducing test anxiety rather than for measuring achievement. Learning thus became more important than certification in the school, and learning meant social interaction, collaboration, argumentation, and discussion. The result was that these students learned not only the material they were studying but discovered reasons for learning it as they complained to teachers and argued with and helped each other.

The Valuation of Skills One of the most important components of the success of the Work Experience Programs was that program participants had available to them a fairly wide range of activities through which they could establish a sense of community with others and also acquire status through the development of individual skill. Some of these activities were associated with the school, but others were part of crew projects or social groupings outside either work or school.

The integration of academic instruction, crew work, and counseling made it possible for participants in the program to accomplish something in any of several ways and have that accomplishment recognized throughout the entire program. The confidence a participant developed from being part of a crew that built a solar greenhouse supported an attempt at something new, such as trying out the school. I saw fulfilled more than the old vocational-education promise that what is learned in class can be of help on the job. Generalized self-esteem and resurgent curiosity grew from the program's recognition of a wide range of skills. Young people who had had only negative experiences with academic education were urged by their crew-mates and friends to give the school a chance. Those who did well in school were challenged by physical labor and trade skills. The teachers, crew supervisors, and counselors worked closely together, and it was obvious to the program participants that these adults had respect for one another's abilities. The examples of adult behavior available to the young people in this program were complex and inclusive.

Adult Models   Because the three major components of Work Experience Programs—counseling, job training, and academic instruction—were well integrated, young participants had a much wider variety of adult models than their peers who remained in high school. In addition, the informality of the school and the crews enabled the young to see adults interacting as full-fledged people in their areas of expertise as well as in other areas, in and outside the school. As noted above, the crews met at the school in the morning before going out on jobs, so new crew members, whether or not they demonstrated interest in working toward a GED, got to know the teachers. Most of the counselors made an effort to see their clients at the school, and thus participants saw another kind of adult work. Students who worked at individual job sites rather than on crews came to know the crew supervisors and saw them at work during school-building renovations. Finally, there were always a number of adult GED students in the school, and they helped the younger students visualize another reality of adult life: coming back to get what was missed before.

The young people in the program saw not only that adults had various skills and areas of expertise but also that adults were not as skillful in some areas as in others. For example, when the crews were working on the school building, the teachers often got involved in the project. Many of us were pretty unskilled carpenters and painters, and it was important for the students to see us deferring to those who knew the business better. Their teachers could hardly be generalized authorities if they had so much to learn. By the same token crew supervisors would bring math, English, or science questions that came up on the job into the school for the teachers to address. Counselors would teach when needed in the school and substitute for crew supervisors on the job. In general, therefore, the artificial distinctions between kinds of work, between official and unofficial positions, and between the young participants and the adults on the staff began to break down, and they were replaced by distinctiveness built on merit, greater knowledge, and finer skill. The social gulfs between staff and participants also began to close. When a crew supervisor went through a divorce, the crew knew something about what was going on and sympathized. When one of the participants got married, several of the teachers and crew supervisors attended the reception.

Because the crews did most of their work for community organizations and social-service agencies, crew members were able to see a cross-section of the city of Fitchburg that would have been impossible had they stayed in high school. In the course of a long job, they could witness the administrative styles of program directors and observe power relationships and relationships between men and women. They saw how they were treated as CETA trainees and could tell who appreciated their work, and who was just seeking free labor.

In one or two cases we were able to involve parents in the program, but by and large our attempts here were feeble and doomed to failure, in large part because so many of the young people in the program came from troubled homes and had parents who had too many problems of their own to get involved with us. As I look back on our work, however, I see that we should have made a greater effort here.

Other Children and the Elderly   The age range in Work Experience Classroom was from sixteen to over sixty. Once we established a credit-sharing and referral network with area school systems, we accepted a few students who were fifteen, or even fourteen, but most of the students in the school were between the ages of sixteen and twenty. Although we did not separate students into classes according to age, we also made no special effort to engage our students with younger children. In one case, a nineteen-year-old graduate of our program worked in a Fitchburg junior high school as a counselor and eventually became a crew supervisor himself in the Neighborhood Youth Corps summer program. But we could have explored a wide range of relationships with the public schools, day-care centers, and nursing homes in the area, had we been aware of how important younger children and the elderly are to an adolescent's construction of meaning in the world and his or her vision of adulthood.

Some of our students had children of their own while they were part of the program, and in most cases their ignorance of baby and child care was shocking. An educational program that involved parents, social-service agencies, and some work with young children might have helped some of these adolescent parents acquire a clearer understanding of their child's needs and their own responsibilities.

Academic Skills   From a traditional educational perspective, the most striking characteristic of Work Experience Classroom was that, with all the job training, counseling sessions, and conversation, virtually every young person who stayed in the school more than two or three months made significant improvements in reading, writing, and math, and many obtained a high school equivalency certificate. The longest a participant could be with the program was eighteen months, and in many cases people came to us reading on a third- or fourth-grade level (based on the Reading for Understanding standardized test) and left eighteen months later with a GED. The most dramatic improvement I saw was in a sixteen-year-old who tested at a second-grade reading level his first week in the school and one year later, when he left the program, was reading on a ninth-grade level. Perhaps the greatest testimony to the school's academic success is that people who heard about the school but were not eligible to participate in a CETA program came voluntarily, without pay, to work on English, reading, writing, and math skills.

Clearly the students were getting enough academic instruction, but more important, they were receiving that instruction in an environment that helped them make sense of it in their personal lives. I am convinced that this meaning made possible the phenomenal leaps of skill we observed. The staff shared an assumption that reading, writing, and math skills were critical to survival and well-being in American society. Our students came to the school on all levels, with various problems and disabilities, but there was no compromise on the need for competence in these areas. Nevertheless, with high standards of competence came reasons, in the form of adult models, for learning how and why to read, write, and do math. The explanations we offered participants in the Work Experience Program were less important than the fact that they could see us, with all our successes, failures, strengths, and weaknesses, working through questions and problems ourselves.

Our greatest achievement in Work Experience Classroom, I believe, was in discarding old assumptions about what was important or praiseworthy in education in favor of paying attention to what the children said and did. This focus enabled us to rebuild our standards on the basis of what we were able to *portray* for our students, what we, as adults, were willing to stand for and defend. We stumbled into the dialogue between adults and children in Work Experience Classroom, little knowing what a remarkable rediscovery we were making.

RING DAY CARE CENTER

Most of the Work Experience Classroom students were adolescents between the ages of fifteen and twenty. At the other end of the educational spectrum, in terms of student age, is the Ring Day Care Center in Springfield, Massachusetts. I learned about this center through the director, Maggie Adams, a student in the University without Walls program at the University of Massachusetts. When I read what Ms. Adams had written about her center I was amazed at the way in which the Ring program seemed to demonstrate the evolutionary principles of children's learning I had been trying for so long to identify. I talked at length with Ms. Adams about the Ring Day Care Center, and in October 1986, I visited the program for half a day. The description below is based on Ms. Adams's writing, our talks, and my brief visit. It is presented not as a comprehensive study of an early-childhood education program but as an example of (1) how paying attention to children's responses, inclinations, and preferences in learning can lead educators to evolutionarily sound principles of teaching and program development and (2) ways in which evolutionary principles of education might be applied.

Ring Day Care Center is located in the Ring Nursing Home in Springfield. The program has been in operation for four years and was developed by Ms. Adams and the director of the nursing home to provide day care for nursing home employees and opportunities for nursing home residents and children to interact. There are presently eighteen children in the center. Nine of these are children of Ring Nursing Home employees, and nine are children from the community who attend on a tuition basis. It is center policy that no more than 50 percent of the slots in the program may be occupied by children from the community at large. The children who attend the center range in age from two years nine months to five years.

The center staff consists of two full-time teachers and Ms. Adams, the director, who is three-quarter time. In addition, the center has acquired the services of two women through the Foster Grandparent Program, student teachers placed by the local community college, and interns from a local vocational high school—all at no cost. The basic costs of the day-care center are salaries and supplies; the nursing home provides space, food service (lunches and snacks), laundry service, and some money for salaries. Additional funds are acquired through tuitions and Aid to Families with Dependent Children day-care vouchers. Interestingly enough, over the course of four years there has been no increase in the total cost to run the nursing home as result of the development of the center.

When I asked Ms. Adams what the most important goals of the center were, she answered without hesitation: "to foster independence and positive self-images by allowing children to choose, by supporting their choices, and by not setting up arbitrary adult standards for children; and to set up the environment so that children are interested in learning and can develop social and emotional skills." Let us examine the center in terms of evolutionary principles to see how these goals are achieved.

Size   Although space considerations have something to do with the number of children in Ring Day Care Center, Ms. Adams acknowledges the importance of keeping the program small. If there were many more than eighteen children in the center, it would be impossible to allow them the kind of self-direction that is such an important part of the Ring philosophy. When there are too many children and not enough staff, the teachers inevitably become more concerned with management than with children's learning.

Power and Participation of Children   Children in the Ring Day Care Center have a tremendous amount of choice in terms of how and with whom they will spend their day. The center staff are acutely conscious of children's needs to make choices and solve problems on their own, so within the framework imposed by nursing home logistics (e.g., lunch is offered at a particular time during the day), everything is done to create an environment that facilitates choice. For example, that old standby of early-childhood education, the nap, is not compulsory at Ring. As Ms. Adams put it, "We don't force the children to take naps. But there are some children who do need them. So we have a time for naps during the day. We also try to make the children who don't need naps sensitive to the needs of others, so we ask for quiet play at this time." The mid-morning snack is simply laid out on a table at the Ring Center, and children choose when they will interrupt what they are doing to eat. The snack table thus becomes a new locus of social activity that the children manage themselves.

At Ring the children have the choice to play by themselves or with others. The environment is set up in such a way, with central tables for group play and little nooks for individuals who need to be alone, that children can flow from one kind of activity to the other without the permission of the adults. Even the morning group meeting or "circle time" is not compulsory, and thus, says Ms. Adams, the meeting becomes something the children *want* to do.

At the same time there are special group activities built around holidays in which all participate. During these celebrations the nursing-home residents come to the center, and there are songs and games for everyone. In addition, at the end of the year the center holds a picnic to which residents and parents are invited.

After talking with Ms. Adams and visiting the center, it was clear to me that the people at Ring have worked hard to establish a dynamic balance between the needs of these children to be part of a group and their equally powerful needs to establish individual identities and investigate the environment. When I entered the center I saw a number of activities going on all at once. For example, three children sat at a table with a foster grandmother, rolling out clay, while three or four others painted at another table. One child was working alone with a teacher on a huge Lego creation, and another was wandering from table to table observing the work of others but not getting involved in any activity. A little boy at the clay table looked up at me as I entered and said, "Hi, we're makin' pizza. You wanna make it with us?" So I sat down and made pizza for a while.

I was struck by the self-confidence and comfort these children demonstrated around a new adult. They asked me questions about what I liked, where I came from, and what I thought was best on pizza. Certainly young children in *any* kind of program have this enthusiasm, curiosity, and energy, but all too often they are made to conform to the program: now it is time for this or that activity; now it is time to be quiet. The learning in many early-childhood programs—especially the academically oriented preschools—is almost wholly structured by adults, and children are disciplined in more or less subtle ways if they do not want to participate. The basic limits at Ring are straightforward and easy for children to understand: do not hurt others, and respect others' work. Perhaps more important, the staff takes pains to explain the reasons for these limits and other rules that are necessary for safety in the nursing home environment.

The Valuation of Skills   The primary emphasis at Ring Day Care Center is not on academic knowledge and skill but on motor and social skills. Certainly if a child demonstrates an interest in books or in drawing or music, these interests are encouraged, but for the most part the Ring center staff see themselves as people who provide an environment for children to *discover*. As Ms. Adams noted in our conversation, this commitment means that teachers and aides support the choices that children make as long as they do not hurt others. As a result the children develop an appreciation for a wide range of skills and inevitably come to understand the criteria of skill.

Adult Models   One of the most striking things about Ring Day Care Center is the connection children have with a variety of adults—teachers, student teachers, foster grandparents, parents, and, of course, the nursing home residents (see below). At least half of these children spend their day in the same building in which their parents work, and the center welcomes informal visits from parents. One child in the center even has a grandfather in the nursing home. Because the children have as much contact as they do with the nursing home residents, they acquire some knowledge of what their parents do on the job and some understanding of the larger context of their work.

The teachers, administrators, volunteers, students, and nursing home employees who spend time with these children over the course of a year provide a more diverse view of adulthood than is usually available in an early childhood education program. The children get to know the maintenance people in the nursing home (who build and maintain most of the furniture, partitions, and other structures of the center), the kitchen staff (the residents and the children often cook together), secretaries, activities coordinators, and nurse's aides.

Other Children and the Elderly   Ring Day Care Center is an inter-generational early-childhood program, and the children spend a good deal of time with the nursing home residents. It is important to note two characteristics of this interaction that have probably contributed greatly to Ring's success with this experiment. First, children are never forced to participate in activities with the residents; they (and the residents, for that matter) volunteer. As with other center activities, therefore, these moments with the residents become special to the children. Indeed, the morning of my visit many more children wanted to make muffins with the elderly resident volunteers than could be accommodated.

Second, the elderly and the children are companions for one another; there is no pretense of instruction, no educational responsibility to burden the residents. They talk together, sing songs, look at books, make things, or cook. The most obvious benefit of this arrangement to the children, from an evolutionary perspective, is that, instead of being completely isolated from the realities of old age and death, they come to accept them as facts of life.

The benefits for the elderly in the Ring Nursing Home cannot be overemphasized. Spending time with the center children helps to provide residents with a sense of connection with the world and with ongoing life. As they come toward their own deaths, they are not isolated or shut away from the rest of society. They can draw a sense of personal value from their interaction with the children.

Work Experience Classroom served adolescents who, for the most part, could have legally dropped out of school, and Ring Day Care Center is a tiny program serving only a handful of young children, their parents, and a group of elderly residents in a nursing home. As noted at the beginning of this chapter, I offer these programs as examples of the range that an evolutionary perspective may have in the evaluation and planning of educational programs for children. Nevertheless, one may wonder whether it is possible to utilize an evolutionary perspective in the vast public school systems, where most children in the United States spend so much of their time between the ages of five and eighteen. Is the only answer, as many have suggested, a wholesale restructuring and "de-schooling" of society? Having the experience I had in Work Experience Classroom and discovering what has been done at the Ring center to faciltiate children's learning have given me a sense that the principles of an evolutionary perspective on children's learning may be applied on any educational level and in any situation. Indeed, there have been large-scale movements in education in recent years that, like the microcosms of a particular alternative school or an inter-generational day-care center, reflect evolutionary principles. The final chapter of this book explores some of these positive directions in children's education and offers some suggestions for integrating an evolutionary perspective into school reform.

13

Promising Directions

ALTHOUGH the picture of public schooling presented in chapter 9 is bleak, a number of educational alternatives have been developed during the past twenty years that give an evolutionist cause for cautious optimism. None of these projects has been explicitly grounded in an evolutionary perspective, but because alternative approaches often explicitly acknowledge the broad socializing function of education, they are usually sensitive to the *child's* responses to the learning environment. Paying attention to how children actually do learn has, as with Work Experience Classroom and Ring Day Care Center, led many of these programs to what I now see as "evolutionary" conclusions concerning how children (and adults, for that matter) learn best.

An evolutionary view of learning provides the theoretical foundation for alternative and community education that has been lacking in the past. It makes unambiguous the price of ignoring natural human learning inclinations. As long as this price remained impressionistic, it was possible for us to discount dropout rates, student unrest, parental confusion, and clear messages from the "conflict paradigm" (Hurn 1985) that formal education is bad for people. But learning by discovery in a democratic social context is a *characteristic of our species*, and we are kidding ourselves if we think that a longer school year, more rigorous basic-skills instruction, higher academic standards, and all the other suggestions that have come out of studies such as *A Nation at Risk* will solve the "education problem" in this country. An evolutionary perspective also makes it clear that, in order for children to learn naturally, they need to have consistent yet varied adult models. Thus we are equally foolish if we believe children will be well served in an environment in which the only adults around are trying to get out of the children's way. Finally, an evolutionary way of looking at educational issues is grounded in the need that all humans have to belong to a group and to be acknowledged as individuals by the other members of the group. It is thus hardly surprising that the more removed children are from their conception of who is in the "band," the greater their distress.

Let us briefly review the alternative- and community-education movements in the United States to see how they have addressed the problems of children's education. An evolutionary perspective here can serve as both a framework for critique and a catalyst for renewed effort.

ALTERNATIVE EDUCATION

The "alternative" feature of a so-called alternative school is usually a commitment to providing more opportunities for children to make decisions about their own learning than exist in traditional schools. To be sure, there are all kinds of "alternative" schools. Some provide virtually no direction from adults, in the Summerhill mode, while other alternatives to public school are strict behavior-modification programs in which all the direction comes from adults. When I use the term *alternative school* here, I am referring to organized educational programs that display the following characteristics.

Successful alternative schools engage students in different kinds of activities—both "vocational" and "academic"—so that the skills learned are varied and the opportunities for acquiring competence and self-confidence are distributed among a greater range of interests and abilities than is common in the public schools (see, e.g., the Channel 1 program in Gloucester, Massachusetts [Gloucester Community Development Corporation, 1981]).

Such schools are usually less formal than the public schools, and children are presented with a much wider spectrum of adult behavior. Because the *process* of education is at least as important as the subject matter in alternative schools, adult opinions, assumptions, and attitudes cannot easily be hidden behind a curriculum. In addition, most alternative schools are small and have a low teacher-student ratio. Thus the children in the school are in a position to get to know one another and the adults on a more individualized and intimate basis.

A popular belief states that the alternative school is dead and that the experiments in education that arose all across the country during the late 1960s and developed through the 1970s are folding one by one, unable to generate the funding necessary to stay open and unable to build support in the community. While a general conservative swing in education has directed criticism against alternative schools (just as it spawned *A Nation at Risk*, the 1983 report of the National Commission on Excellence in Education), it is also true that alternative schools and alternative educational philosophies have had a profound impact on the lives of large numbers of children and on the educational establishment itself.

There is some evidence that children in alternative educational programs do about as well academically (measured by standardized tests) as children in more traditional schools (see, e.g., Smith, Gregory, and Pugh 1981). As Hurn (1985) points out, this observation also means that children who attend alternative schools do not do any *better*, in traditional academic terms, than children who attend regular schools, but it is important to note that the additional attention to process and community usually present in alternative schools does not seem to have a negative effect on academic achievement. In Work Experience Classroom, where adolescents actually spent less time working on, say, math yet learned the subject at least as well as they had in junior high and high school.

More important than standardized academic achievement, for the purposes of learning identified in this book, children often leave an alternative-learning experience with broader-based, more generalizable skills and with a heightened sense of personal confidence and competence (see Raywid 1981). The fact that children attending alternative schools are often those who have not been able to succeed (measured in any way) in a traditional public school makes this evidence all the more compelling. If an alternative school can generate enthusiasm for learning in children who have had negative educational experiences, something worth paying attention to is going on.

Although a number of alternative schools have closed down in recent years, a far larger number have been incorporated into public school systems as "official" alternatives.

> From [their] beginning 10 years ago, public alternative schools have grown from 100 or so in 1970 to more than 10,000 today. Alternatives are found in 80% of the nation's larger school districts (those enrolling 25,000 or more students), and they have begun to appear even in the smallest districts: One out of every five districts enrolling fewer than 600 students now claims one or more alternatives. An estimated three million U.S. youngsters are currently enrolled in alternative programs. (Raywid 1981, 552)

As with school reform in general (see Chapter 11), this phenomenon can be seen from different points of view, depending on one's frame of reference. From one perspective the incorporation of the alternative school or the principles of alternative education into public schools represents a co-opting of the critique of public education that the alternative schools embodied. From this point of view these schools have been absorbed by the larger educational culture in the same way other individuals and organizations critical of the cultural establishment have been absorbed. In the process of mainstreaming, these alternative critiques have been weakened or deflected, and what is called an alternative program in a public school may in actuality be nothing more than a dumping ground for troublesome children.

Although such programs exist, the overall evidence justifies a more optimistic view. If many school systems across the country are adopting alternative programs and if teachers, administrators, parents, and school-board members are becoming aware that children need a wider range of options, it is a sign that the educational establishment itself is in flux. The incorporation of some alternative programming in the public schools may reflect a more realistic understanding of the socialization responsibilities of the school and as such may serve as a basis for future critique and experimentation.

COMMUNITY EDUCATION

There are two serious problems associated with alternative schools—
problems that Work Experience Classroom never solved. The first is the
same problem that has always plagued educational alternatives that try
to deal with the whole environment of learning: children in such schools
are often socialized only for the environment of the school. I certainly
saw this problem occur time and again in Work Experience Classroom.
Adolescents who were able to expand their behavioral repertoire and their
self-discipline in the school were unable to exercise these skills in their
families or their peer groups. A student who showed genuine concern
for others on the job stole a car one weekend; two students who had built
some self-confidence in the school overdosed on drugs and alcohol one
night and nearly died. This very problem, of course, makes it tempting
to hide an alternative school in the country and *create* the total learning
community. But such a move is not the answer. The larger learning
community will always be waiting, and most alternative-school
graduates, like most prisoners, will want to come back to people and
places they know.

The second problem with alternative schools is similar to the first but
is on an organizational level. Alternative programs that are not integrated
into the community or communities they are part of are incredibly vulnerable.

Work Experience Classroom made some progress toward collaboration with public schools, chambers of commerce, local colleges, and
social-service agencies in the CETA Consortium. We negotiated credit-
sharing arrangements and created a referral network with six school
districts in the area. The school was part of an Inter-Agency Council, an
informal (and, unfortunately, short-lived) group made up of Fitchburg
organizations that worked with or were concerned about adolescents. But
we could not establish the school as an integral part of Fitchburg and
other Montachusett Region communities in time to prevent its collapse.
The school did not belong to the communities it served. It was funded
solely by federal money and was part of the CETA organization. When
CETA priorities began to change and money became tight, it thus was
impossible to have a public discussion about the fate of the school. Work

Experience Classroom slid from view with hardly a murmur of protest, even though the school was fulfilling an important community function.

The community-education movement offers some approaches to these problems of isolation and vulnerability that make good sense when viewed from an evolutionary perspective. The major assumption of community education is that many individuals and organizations that have nothing to do with formal schooling are definitely engaged in education. The community educator's job is to bring these efforts together and help make their educational function manifest. In this vision of education, any agency, any organization, or activity may serve as an educational resource, and anyone in the community may have something valuable to teach others. From an evolutionary perspective the goals of community education match up very well with the needs of children for a wider range of adult models, a broader conception of skill and knowledge, more opportunities to distinguish oneself, and a clearer sense of the meaning of adult life.

One of the most exciting things about the community-education movement is that in recent years there has been a trend toward integrating both individual and collective goals and education and learning.

> The first of these trends is the shift from community education as "school-community relations" to "education-community relations." The movement now sees the school as one, but only one, of the educational agencies in one community. . . .
>
> The second trend involves a shift in the purposes of community education. The major objective heretofore has been individual growth and development. Currently, increasing emphasis is being put on community development as co-equal in importance. . . .
>
> The third trend involves conceptualizing community education more importantly as a process than as groups of programs or products. (Fantini, Loughran, and Reed 1980, 11)

These trends in community education clearly represent a perception of the basic unity of the human need to be part of a community and also to achieve as an individual. What is the *process* of learning in a community if it is not discovery, interaction, exploration, and identification? A public school that is involved in community education encourages the participation of parents and other community members in *every* aspect of the school, from curriculum development to teaching to budgeting and politicking. Children in such a school spend only part of their time in the school building. The rest of the time they are learning from community members—observing their work, their meetings, their solutions to problems, their skill and lack of skill. Adults who are community educators (rather than professional educators) volunteer their time and energy because they know how important it is for children to see a broad spectrum of adult activity and to integrate formal education with other experience.

PROBLEMS IN COMMUNITY EDUCATION

The trends in community education are encouraging and represent avenues through which an evolutionary perspective may be applied and evaluated. But the problems of community education are many, and it is important to touch on some of them here because they are also problems associated with the application of an evolutionary perspective to children's learning.

One of the most difficult tasks of community education is knowing what the community is. This identifying and defining process is often called "community development." As noted in chapter 8, today's large societies are typically pluralistic confederations in which hundreds or even thousands of subcommunities may exist. Does the term *community education* imply an identification with a political entity—a town or city? Certainly the political unit has great power in our society—power to appropriate funds, to attract money from larger political units, to make decisions that affect subgroups. But community education implies a wide variety of groups that may or may not be permanent, that may have only a single issue in common, and that may in fact be pitted against the political unit. In the small Massachusetts town I live in, people have a plethora of allegiances that only occasionally overlap.

The failure to identify the community for which community-education processes are devised can create serious problems. First, it is easy for community-education programs to get caught in an impossible attempt to provide something for every need in every community. In this situation either the focus of the project becomes hopelessly diffused and the activities fragmented, or the program falls prey to rigid structure and quantitative evaluation. Second, if it is perceived by some groups in the community at large that a community education activity is intended for a particular, different constituency, chances are they will withhold their support.

An evolutionary perspective allows us to see that beneath the apparent dissimilarity of immediate needs and attitudes in any society are deep emotional needs that are common to all human beings. This view suggests that, when the activities and ideas of a community project are formed with these commonalities in mind, the project can actually unite disparate groups and provide the basis for community integration at a higher level (or, more properly, a reintegration at a deeper level).

One such activity could be children's education, because it is something all people in the community are concerned about—either because they have children in school or because they are paying for it. But applying an evolutionary perspective to a public discussion on children's education is an extremely difficult task.

The debate between individual fulfillment and collective need that has characterized public schooling in the United States since its inception reflects the great schism in our society between belonging to a group and defining individual identity, noted in chapter 8. I have tried to present the case that these characteristics of human sociality are naturally in balance, not in conflict; the emphasis on individual aggrandizement in our society, however, makes the reestablishment of this balance a monumental task. Many parents in United States society tend to think of a school less as part of the community than as a place in which *their child* receives basic skills instruction and is cared for during the day. Those who have no children in school are more likely to see the school as the agency that raises their taxes rather than the agency through which they can participate in the education of the community's children.

Building a consciousness of community, particularly in the United States, is probably more difficult than anyone wants to admit, and the task may imply a level of abstraction that most community educators would like to avoid. The ideas that unite members of a foraging band into The People certainly exist at some level of abstraction, but these ideas are inextricably connected with the natural environment and with blood and marriage ties. There is no separation between the idea and the people one actually sees on a day-to-day basis. In larger societies, and especially in pluralistic societies like the United States, the idea of community consists of elements that are only vaguely related to the natural environment, if at all, and are only distantly related to kinship.

Large societies have to characterize their communality in increasingly abstract terms so that large numbers of unrelated people in different environments can find some emotional connection with one another in their often gratuitous association. The notions of The People represented by "Christianity" or "the Irish" or "the town of Shutesbury" may surely be emotionally charged, and they may serve to fulfill the fundamental needs of belonging and participation—even of individual importance. But they also require a kind of intellectual or metaphysical effort that unites people through language and imagination. I have been on the school board in the town of Shutesbury for more than two years, and I can testify that it takes real effort and imagination for those who do not have children in school to acknowledge their responsibility for the education of the community's children.

This intellectualization of belonging is a relatively new problem for human beings, one that has grown as ethnic attachments have had less and less to do with real kin and reciprocal obligations have become abstracted and quantified. Perhaps it is time for us to to create a vision of The People that acknowledges the old balances but also extends membership in the band to a global society.

Because the tradition of individuality is so powerful in our society, a given community-education process—a parent cooperative day-care center, for example, or a community basketball league—is often built around the abilities, talents, and concerns of specific individuals who, in effect, "own" the idea. It is disconcerting to think of the number of times good programs have broken down simply because the people in whom so much responsibility was vested departed, and those who remained had not had a full share in the vision. Charismatic leadership has its advantages and disadvantages, I suppose, but at the risk of oversimplifying, the most successful community-education project, for the long run, will be the one that learns a lesson from nomadic foraging societies: group stability implies a diffusion of leadership and the widest possible participation of members. In this way reliance on specific individuals may be reduced, and the organization itself may become more like a community.

EDUCATION FOR SYNTHESIS

An ironic twist to an evolutionary perspective concerns the relationship between intellectual skill—developed to a highly specialized degree in the course of civilization—and emotional needs that have often been ignored in the headlong rush to implement the productions of our detached minds. This irony is present in the above discussion where it was proposed that a high level of abstraction (The People as global society) is necessary to enable us to reestablish social balances that have been disrupted in human history largely through increased abstraction. Is this proposal an impossible contradiction? Let us examine this aspect of the evolutionary perspective in more detail.

Nomadic foraging societies and the societies of higher primates provide for the collective and individual needs of their members simultaneously because the way of life itself maintains the balance. There is nothing inherently good or moral about living life this way, but the intimate connection with the physical environment makes cooperation essential, makes sharing advantageous, and encourages individuals to seek status and importance in the context of what is also best for the whole group. As human beings we are adapted to environments in which these relationships are not only possible but rewarded. The physical world and our dependence on it, however, have changed so dramatically in the past ten thousand years that the balances characteristic of nomadic foraging societies will not simply reemerge if we construct educational and social activities that emphasize emotional needs. Though we cannot afford to ignore our biologically based social and learning inclinations, neither can we rely on them.

An evolutionary perspective suggests that human beings carry within themselves deeply rooted needs and inclinations that play out in different ways according to the environment in which they must be realized. In the original social environment these needs and inclinations mediated a balance between the group and the individual, between men and men, women and women, men and women, parents and children, sibling and sibling, old and young. But in other environments there is no telling what they might mediate.

In the absence of natural direction from the environment, we must provide our own, and in order for many people in large societies to share these understandings, they must be in the form of abstract ideas. These ideas need not be new or original, and they may not be directly associated with specific needs of specific communities, but they must be large concepts, what Bruner calls "great organizing ideas, ideas that inevitably stem from deeper values and points of view about man and nature" (1979, 120). They must be thoughts that can capture imagination and allow a considerable amount of room for individual interpretation and practical application within and among subgroups in a society.

Getting people together is a commendable activity, but we have gone so far along the line of specialization and abstraction that we often do not realize the purpose of our getting together unless we are threatened or have a gripe in common. Humans living in the twentieth century are victims of a kind of cognitive hypertrophy, but these overdeveloped intellectual mechanisms are now critical to survival in the new environment. If for millennia our intellectual systems have led us away from some of the most important characteristics of being human, these same intellectual systems must lead us back again.

Survival and well-being in the modern world demand cognitive competence and a command of intellectual skills such as reading, writing, and logico-mathematical reasoning. While these skills need not be acquired in a repressive learning environment, they nevertheless require considerable practice in an environment that demonstrates to children that they are valuable. Children (and their teachers, their families, and other community members) need to have common ideas about academic education—ideas that make clear connections between the need for academic skill and other, more ancient needs.

Schools reenter the picture at this point. Some have advocated the "deschooling of society" (e.g., Illich 1970; Kozol 1975), but the schools must be included in any attempt to reconceive our humanness and implement the perspectives that grow from that reconception. I do not believe that the formal education can be the *spearhead* of social change in the United States, as Brameld hoped in the late 1950s. The Revisionists have shown that schools in this country are cultural institutions that, in general, reflect the values and perceived needs of the dominant culture. But the reconception is already underway. The remarkable appearance of "human-resource development" departments and "quality circles" in American business and industry may be seen as an acknowledgment (belated, grudging, and forced by sagging profits as it may be) of human needs simultaneously to belong and to be important as individuals. It is crucial that these experiments be seen in a context larger than the next quarter's earnings, and the schools can help enlarge and interpret that context for children and adults alike.

Precisely because the schools are cultural institutions they are essential to the endeavor to recover our humanness. As noted above, they already provide focal points for community building. People continue to care about and get involved in what happens to their children, and local funding of public schools ensures the participation of everyone in the community — at least on one level. Potentially integrative structures, such as the school board and the PTA, are already in place in most school systems throughout the country. Finally, institutions of formal education are traditionally seen as the repository for the kinds of selection, synthesizing, and expressive skills that are critical to the empowerment of individuals and the cohesiveness of communities on any level in modern society. Even though schools have not conveyed these skills to children as well as we might like, most people still believe that school is the only place they can be obtained. And there is some truth in this view.

Of course, if the schools are to help people in a community define problems, create larger contexts for understanding problems, and locate the resources to solve them, the schools themselves must change. Currently the schools (especially the secondary schools) expose children to ambiguity and uncertainty without helping them acquire the skills of linking and analyzing ideas and experiences. This kind of education condemns them to fear and mistrust. Any self-reliance that emerges from such a learning environment must of necessity be narrow and defensive — a self-reliance that eschews reciprocal obligation and contributes to isolation and self-centeredness. Schools are institutions essentially cut off from their communities, in spite of well-meaning attempts to "involve parents" from time to time. Indeed, as noted in chapter 9, because teachers are so poorly paid, they have an investment in making their knowledge arcane and creating the impression that children will suffer without their expertise. Nevertheless, an evolutionary perspective can help us focus the achievements of alternative and community education. Within the new framework that emerges from this focus, the school grows into a kind of community resource center and the teacher becomes a maker of connections, a demonstrator, and a magician.

Here we have run into John Dewey again and one of the ideas that may serve to integrate modern and ancient needs. According to Dewey (e.g.,[1938] 1963), "educative experience" leads to increasingly complex and inclusive understanding—of an activity or of a community. When a carpenter estimates the cost and timing of a large job, when a cook plans a complex meal, or when a scholar writes a book, there are a number of both cognitive and emotional processes at work. Regardless of the particular area in which they are being exercised, these processes are much alike. They involve the perception and interpretation of pattern, the integration of several different kinds of information, the identification of problems, and the making of decisions. As noted in chapter 11, Dewey believed that helping children understand these systems was the primary function of education in a democracy and insisted that, as children learned about their own experiences and the experiences of others, a bond of understanding would grow in the learning community. Developing a theoretical framework for their experiences would enable children to extend their skill, to enter into unfamiliar territory with less apprehension, and to tolerate greater ambiguity and diversity as the world changed around them.

The school is part of a larger community, and it must be more than the place where children acquire academic information and skill. The school must do more than *present* these things to children; it must make the case for them—to the whole community—and offer opportunities for people to use them profitably.

Such a school can pose the large questions. We need to know about how human interaction has changed with the development of large societies, with the acceptance and expectation of change, the burgeoning information systems, and the development of large-scale competition. Children growing up in a technological society need to know what power is and what forms it can take. They need to know where rules come from and why it is often easier to obey them rather than fight them. It is important for them to acquire an understanding of why they feel bad when they are not acknowledged by others and why success is hollow if it is not shared. Children need to get hold of integrating ideas, conceptions that link human beings to one another and to other life on earth. The schools should not be held responsible for all the learning children do, but if children are learning more in their communities and if education begins with skills that all can hold in common, the schools can help children, their parents, and others integrate and interpret learning through the skills of thinking and expression. In such a school teachers become less specialized, less focused on content, and more like community educators. The specialized knowledge they do have is more like that of a leader in a group—knowledge of how to bring a group to a consensus, and of how to involve others and knowledge of the problems faced by the community and its individual members and how these problems are connected with the great ideas in history, scientific discovery, art, and literature.

In a community of learners that is attempting to understand the commonalities of human experience and the connections of human beings with other forms of life, tolerance, cooperation, and an appreciation for the experience of others may indeed develop. In such a community individuals may gain greater power to influence the decisions that are made concerning them by extending their skill and competence into new areas and by making connections between pieces of information that may have been forbidding and unknown in the past. At the same time such a learning community can help individuals become responsible members of a group, that is, people who incorporate an understanding of the human need for belonging and participation into any power and influence they wield. Finally, people living and learning in such an environment will draw pleasure and satisfaction from the learning process itself because the process will be grounded in what is important to them.

Perhaps it is naive to hope for (much less demand) the implementation of social and educational reforms that are "evolutionary" rather than merely "revolutionary." There are so many special interests, so much threat and supposed threat in our society at present, that it is extraordinarily difficult for people to unite. But what is so appealing about looking at things from an evolutionary perspective is that it may inform our thought on any level—in any classroom, any school-board meeting, and any community. It may form the agenda of a study group, provide a counterpoint at a faculty conference, offer a teacher exciting alternatives for curriculum development, or guide the reformation of a junior high school. An evolutionary perspective knits together a number of ideas that have been disconnected—even seemingly contradictory—in the past. It locates us and our children in the great story of life on earth and offers a framework that can assist our attempts to understand our interactions and, from our understanding, create environments in which our interactions are more cooperative, productive, and equitable. There is no going back, but an evolutionary perspective can help us go on.

References

Ardrey, Robert. 1966. *The Territorial Imperative*. New York: Atheneum.

Auel, Jean M. 1980. *The Clan of the Cave Bear*. New York: Bantam.

Baldwin, J. D., and J. I. Baldwin. 1979. "The Phylogenetic and Ontogenetic Variables That Shape Behavior and Social Organization." In *Primate Ecology and Human Origins: Ecological Influences on Social Organization*, edited by I. S. Bernstein and E. O. Smith. New York: Garland STPM Press.

Balikci, Asen. 1970. *The Netsilik Eskimo*. Garden City, N.Y.: Natural History Press.

Berndt, Catherine H. 1981. "Interpretations and 'Facts' in Aboriginal Australia." In *Woman the Gatherer*, edited by F. Dahlberg. New Haven: Yale University Press.

Biesele, M. 1976. "Aspects of !Kung Folklore." In *Kalahari Hunter-Gatherers*, edited by R. Lee and I. DeVore. Cambridge: Harvard University Press.

Birdsell, J. 1968. "Some Predictions for the Pleistocene Based on Equilibrium Systems among Recent Hunter-Gatherers." In *Man the Hunter*, edited by R. Lee and I. DeVore. New York: Aldine.

Blurton Jones, N., and M. Konner. 1976. "!Kung Knowledge of Animal Behavior." In *Kalahari Hunter-Gatherers*, edited by R. Lee and I. DeVore. Cambridge: Harvard University Press.

Boesch, C., and H. Boesch. 1981. "Sex Differences in the Use of Natural Hammers by Wild Chimpanzees: A Preliminary Report." *Journal of Human Evolution* 10:585–93.

Boocock, Sarane. 1980. *Sociology of Education: An Introduction*. Boston: Houghton Mifflin.

Bowles, S., and H. Gintis. 1974. "If John Dewey Calls . . . Tell Him Things Didn't Work Out." *Journal of Open Education*, 2 (2): 1–17.

——. 1976. *Schooling in Capitalist America*. New York: Basic Books.

Brameld, T. 1956. *Toward a Reconstructed Philosophy of Education*. New York: Dryden.

Briggs, J. 1970. *Never in Anger*. Cambridge: Harvard University Press.

——. 1979. "Aspects of Inuit Value Socialization." In *National Museum of Man*. Canadian Ethology Service, No. 56. Ottawa: National Museums of Canada.

Bruner, J. 1971. *The Relevance of Education*. New York: Norton.

——. 1977. *The Process of Education*. Cambridge: Harvard University Press.

——. 1979. *On Knowing: Essays for the Left Hand*. Cambridge: Harvard University Press. See chapters entitled "The Act of Discovery" and "After John Dewey, What?"

Butler, R. A. 1965. "Investigative Behavior." In *Behavior of Nonhuman Primates*, edited by A. M. Schreier, H. F. Harlow, and F. Stolnitz. New York: Academic Press.

Callahan, R. E. 1962. *Education and the Cult of Efficiency*. Chicago: University of Chicago Press.

Caplan, Arthur, ed. 1978. *The Sociobiology Debate*. New York: Harper Colophon.

Chance, M. R. A., and C. J. Jolly. 1970. *Social Groups of Monkeys, Apes, and Man*. New York: Dutton.

Coleman, James. 1961. *The Adolescent Society: The Social Life of the Teenager and Its Impact on Education*. New York: Free Press.

Dahlberg, Frances, ed. 1981. *Woman the Gatherer*. New Haven: Yale University Press.

Darwin, Charles. [1859] 1979. *The Origin of Species*. New York: Avenel.

——. [1872] 1965. *The Expression of the Emotions in Man and Animals*. Chicago: University of Chicago Press.

Dawkins, Richard. 1976. *The Selfish Gene*. New York: Oxford University Press.

DeLacey, P. R. 1970. "A Cross-Cultural Study of Classificatory Ability in Australia." *Journal of Cross-Cultural Psychology* 1 (4): 293–304.

——. 1971. "Classificatory Ability and Verbal Intelligence among High-Contact Aboriginal and Low Socio-Economic White Australian Children." *Journal of Cross-Cultural Psychology* 2 (4): 393–96.

DeVore, I., ed. 1965. *Primate Behavior*. New York: Holt, Rinehart, Winston.

Dewey, John. [1916] 1961. *Democracy and Education*. New York: Macmillan.

——. [1938] 1963. *Experience and Education*. New York: Macmillan, Collier Books.

——. 1956. *The Child and the Curriculum, The School and Society*. Chicago: University of Chicago Press.

Dobzhansky, T. G. 1955. *Evolution, Genetics and Man*. New York: Wiley.

Dolhinow, P. J., and N. Bishop. 1970. "The Development of Motor Skills and Social Relationships among Primates through Play." In *Minnesota Symposia on Child Psychology*, edited by J. P. Hill. Minneapolis: University of Minnesota Press.

Draper, P. 1976. "Social and Economic Constraints on Child Life Among the !Kung." In *Kalahari Hunter-Gatherers*, edited by R. Lee and I. DeVore. Cambridge: Harvard University Press.

Dreeben, Robert. 1968. *On What Is Learned in School*. Reading, Mass.: Addison-Wesley.

Eibl-Eibesfeldt, I. 1971. *Love and Hate: The Natural History of Behavior Patterns*. New York: Holt, Rinehart and Winston.

Ellefson, J. O. 1968. "Territorial Behavior in the Common White-Handed Gibbon, *Hylobates par lun*." In *Primates: Studies in Adaptation and Variability*, edited by P. Jay. New York: Holt, Rinehart and Winston.

Erikson, E. 1963. *Childhood and Society*. New York: Norton.

———. 1968. *Identity: Youth and Crisis*. New York: Norton.

Fantini, M., B. Loughran, and H. Reed. 1980. "Community Education for the 1980's: A Need for Theory and Research." *Community Education Journal* 10:11–18.

Firth, M., and H. Reed, eds. 1982. *Lifelong Learning Manual: Training for Effective Education in Organizations*. Amherst: University of Massachusetts, Community Education Resource Center.

Fishbein, Harold. 1979. *Evolution, Development, and Children's Learning*. Pacific Palisades, Calif.: Goodyear Publishing.

Gilligan, Carol. 1982. *In a Different Voice: Psychological Theory and Women's Development*. Cambridge: Harvard University Press.

Ginsburg, H., and S. Opper. 1979. *Piaget's Theory of Intellectual Development*. Englewood Cliffs, N. J.: Prentice-Hall.

Giroux, Henry. 1983. *Theory and Resistance in Education: A Pedagogy for Opposition*. South Hadley, Mass.: Bergin and Garvey.

Gloucester Community Development Corporation. 1981. "Channel One Is Your Community." Gloucester, Mass.: Gloucester Community Development Corporation.

Goodale, Jane C. 1971. *Tiwi Wives: A Study of the Women of Melville Island, North Australia*. Seattle: University of Washington Press.

Goodman, Paul. 1970. *Summerhill For and Against*. New York: Hart Publishing.

Gould, Stephen J. 1978. *Ever Since Darwin*. New York: Norton.

Hall, K. R. L., and I. DeVore. 1965. "Baboon Social Behavior." In *Primate Behavior*, edited by I. DeVore. New York: Holt, Rinehart and Winston.

Hamburg, David. 1963. "Emotions in the Perspective of Human Evolution." In *Expression of the Emotions in Man*, edited by P. Knapp. New York: International Universities.

Harding, R. S. O., and G. Teleki. 1981. *Omnivorous Primates: Gathering and Hunting in Human Evolution*. New York: Columbia University Press.

Harlow, H. F., and M. K. Harlow. 1965. "The Affectional Systems." In *Behavior of Non-Human Primates*, edited by A. M. Schrier, H. F. Harlow and F. Stolnitz, vol. 2. New York: Academic Press.

Harlow, H. F., and C. Mears. 1979. *The Human Model: Primate Perspectives*. New York: Wiley.

Hart, C. W. M., and A. R. Pilling. 1979. *The Tiwi of North Australia*. New York: Holt, Rinehart and Winston.

Helm, June. 1961. *The Lynx Point People: The Dynamics of a Northern Athapaskan Band*. National Museum of Canada Bulletin, no. 176. Ottawa.

Henry, Jules. 1963. *Culture against Man*. New York: Vintage.

Holmes, T. H. and R. H. Rahe. 1967. "The Social Readjustment Rating Scale." *Journal of Psychosomatic Research* 11:213–18.

Holt, John. 1964. *How Children Fail*. New York: Pittman.

———. 1967. *How Children Learn*. New York: Pittman.

———. 1970. *Summerhill For and Against*. New York: Hart Publishing.

Hurn, C. 1985. *The Limits and Possibilities of Schooling: An Introduction to the Sociology of Education*. Boston: Allyn and Bacon.

Hutchins, R. M. 1936. *The Higher Learning in America*. New Haven: Yale University Press.

Illich, Ivan. 1970. *Deschooling Society*. New York: Harper and Row.

Isaac, Glynn. 1978. "The Food-Sharing Behavior of Protohuman Hominids." *Scientific American* 238 (14): 90–100.

Itani, J. 1958. "On the Acquisition and Propagation of a New Food Habit in the Troop of Japanese Monkeys at Tashasakiyama." *Primates* 1:85–98.

———. 1972. "A Preliminary Essay on the Relationship between Social Organization and Incest Avoidance in Nonhuman Primates." In *Primate Socialization*, edited by F. E. Poirier. New York: Random House.

Jackson, Phillip. 1968. *Life in Classrooms*. New York: Holt, Rinehart and Winston.

Johanson, Donald, and M. S. Edey. 1981. *Lucy: The Beginnings of Humankind*. New York: Simon and Schuster.

Kagan, J., H. A. Moss, and I. E. Sigel. 1963. "Psychological Significance of Styles of Conceptualization." In *Basic Cognitive Processes in Children*, edited by J. C. Wright and J. Kagan. New York: Society for Research in Child Development.

Katz, Michael. 1975. *Class, Bureaucracy, and Schools*. New York: Praeger.

Katz, Richard. 1976. "Education for Transcendence." In *Kalahari Hunter-Gatherers*, edited by R. Lee and I. DeVore. Cambridge: Harvard University Press.

———. 1982. *Boiling Energy*. Cambridge: Harvard University Press.

Kawai, M. 1965. "Newly Acquired Pre-Cultural Behavior of the Natural Troop of Japanese Monkeys on Koshima Islet." *Primates* 6:1–30.

Kawamura, S. 1958. "Matriarchial Social Ranks in the Minor B Troop: A Study of the Social Rank System in Japanese Monkeys." *Primates* 1:335–91.

Klemp, George O. 1977. "Three Factors of Success." In *Relating Work and Education: Current Issues in Higher Education*, edited by D.W. Vermilye. San Francisco: Jossey-Bass.

Kohlberg, L. 1969. "Stage and Sequence: The Cognitive Development Approach to Socialization." In *Handbook of Socialization Theory and Research*, edited by D. Goslin. Chicago: Rand McNally.

Konner, M. 1976. "Maternal Care, Infant Behavior, and Development among the !Kung." In *Kalahari Hunter-Gatherers*, edited by R. Lee and I. DeVore. Cambridge: Harvard University Press.

Koyama, N. 1970. "Changes in Dominance Rank and Division of a Wild Japanese Monkey Troop in Arashiyama." *Primates* 11:335–91.

Kozol, Jonathan. 1975. *The Night Is Dark and I Am Far from Home*. New York: Bantam.

Kuhn, Thomas. 1970. *The Structure of Scientific Revolutions*. 2d ed. Chicago: University of Chicago Press.

Kummer, Hans. 1971. *Primate Societies: Group Techniques of Ecological Adaptation*. Chicago: Aldine.

———. 1979. "On the Value of Social Relationships to Non-Human Primates: A Heuristic Scheme." In *Human Ecology*, edited by M. von Cranach, K. Foppa, W. Lepenies, and D. Ploog. Cambridge: Cambridge University Press.

Lancaster, Jane B. 1971. "Play-Mothering: The Relations Between Juvenile Females and Young Infants Among Free-Ranging Vervet Monkeys (*Ceropithecus aethiops*)." *Folia Primatologica* 15:161–82.

———. 1975. *Primate Behavior and the Emergence of Human Culture*. New York: Holt, Rinehart and Winston.

Lawick-Goodall, Jane van. 1965. "Chimpanzees of the Gombe Stream Reserve." In *Primate Behavior*, edited by I. DeVore. New York: Holt, Rinehart and Winston.

———. 1971. *In the Shadow of Man*. New York: Houghton Mifflin.

Lee, Richard B. 1979. *The !Kung San: Men, Women and Work in a Foraging Society*. Cambridge: Cambridge University Press.

Lee, Richard, and Irven DeVore, eds. 1968. *Man the Hunter*. New York: Aldine.

——. 1976. *Kalahari Hunter-Gatherers*. Cambridge: Harvard University Press.

Lewis, J. K., and G. P. Sackett. 1980. "Toward an Ontogenetic Monkey Model of Behavioral Development." In *The Evolution of Human Social Behavior*, edited by J. Lockard. New York: Elsevier.

Lorenz, Konrad. 1966. *On Aggression*. New York: Harcourt, Brace and World.

Lovejoy, C. Owen. 1981. "The Origin of Man." *Science* 211 (4480):341–50.

McGrew, W. C. 1979. "Evolutionary Implications of Sex Differences in Chimpanzee Predation and Tool Use." *Perspectives on Human Evolution: The Great Apes*, vol. 5, edited by D. Hamburg and E. McCowan. Menlo Park, Calif.: Cummings Publishing.

MacLean, P. D. 1973. Clarence M. Hincks Memorial Lectures, 1969. In *A Triune Concept of the Brain and Behavior*, edited by T. J. Boag and D. Campbell. Toronto: University of Toronto Press.

Maddock, Kenneth. 1972. *The Australian Aborigines: A Portrait of Their Society*. Baltimore: Penguin.

Marshall, L. 1976. "Sharing, Talking and Giving: Relief of Social Tensions among the !Kung." In *Kalahari Hunter-Gatherers*, edited by R. Lee and I. DeVore. Cambridge: Harvard University Press.

Mead, Margaret. 1970. *Culture and Commitment*. Garden City, N.Y.: Natural History Press.

Meggitt, M. J. 1962. *Desert People*. Sydney: Angus and Robertson.

Messick, S. 1976. *Cognitive Style*. San Francisco: Jossey-Bass.

Modgil, Sohan. 1974. *Piagetian Research*. London: NFER Publishing.

Morris, Desmond. 1967. *The Naked Ape*. New York: McGraw-Hill.

National Commission on Excellence in Education. 1983. *A Nation at Risk: The Imperative for Educational Reform*. Washington, D.C.: U.S. Department of Education.

Neill, A. S. 1960. *Summerhill: A Radical Approach to Childrearing*. New York: Hart Publishing.

Piaget, J. 1952. *The Origins of Intelligence in Children*. Translated by M. Cook. New York: International University Press.

——. 1971. *Biology and Knowledge*. Translated by Beatrix Walsh. Chicago: University of Chicago Press.

——. 1973. *To Understand Is to Invent: The Future of Education*. New York: Grossman.

——. 1976. *Behavior and Evolution*. New York: Pantheon Books.

——. 1980. *Adaptation and Intelligence*. Translated by Stewart Eames. Chicago: University of Chicago Press.

Price-Williams, D. R. 1961. "A Study concerning Concepts of Conservation of Quantity among Primitive Children." *Acta Psychologia* 18:297–305.

———. 1975. *Exploration in Cross-Cultural Psychology.* San Francisco: Chandler and Sharp.

Raywid, M. A. 1981. "The First Decade of Public School Alternatives." *Phi Delta Kappan*, April 1981, 551–54.

Rowell, T. E. 1969. "Long-Term Changes in a Population of Ugandan Baboons." *Folia Primatologia* 11:241–54.

Sade, D. S. 1965. "Some Aspects of Parent-Offspring and Sibling Relations in a Group of Rhesus Monkeys, with a Discussion of Grooming." *American Journal of Physical Anthropology* 23:1–18.

Sahlins, M. 1968. "Notes on the Original Affluent Society." In *Man the Hunter*, edited by R. Lee and I. DeVore. New York: Aldine.

Sarich, Vincent M. 1968. "The Origin of the Hominids: An Immunological Approach." In *Perspectives on Human Evolution*, edited by S. Washburn and P. Jay. New York: Holt, Rinehart and Winston.

Schebesta, P. 1927. *Among the Forest Dwarfs of Malaya.* London: Hutchinson University Library.

Shostak, Marjorie. 1981. *Nisa: The Life and Words of a !Kung Woman.* Cambridge: Harvard University Press.

Silberman, C. 1970. *Crisis in the Classroom.* New York: Random House.

Smith, G. R., T. B. Gregory, and R. C. Pugh. 1981. "Meeting Student Needs: Evidence for the Superiority of Alternative Schools." *Phi Delta Kappan*. April 1981, 561–64.

Spencer, Herbert. 1870–72. *The Principles of Psychology.* 2d ed. 2 vols. London: Williams and Norgate.

Spring, Joel. 1976. *The Sorting Machine: National Educational Policy since 1945.* New York: McKay.

Strehlow, T. G. H. 1970. "Geography and the Totemic Landscape in Central Australia: A Functional Study." In *Australian Aboriginal Anthropology*, edited by R. Berndt. Nedlands, Western Australia: University of Australia Press.

Strum, S. 1981. "Processes and Products of Change: Baboon Predatory Behavior at Gilgil, Kenya." In *Omnivorous Primates*, edited by R.S.O. Harding and G. Teleki. New York: Columbia University Press.

Teleki, Geza. 1974. "Chimpanzee Subsistence Technology: Materials and Skills." *Journal of Human Evolution* 3: 575–94.

———. 1981. "The Omnivorous Diet and Eclectic Feeding Habits of Chimpanzees in Gombe National Park, Tanzania." In *Omnivorous Primates*, edited by R. S. O. Harding and G. Teleki. New York: Columbia University Press.

Tinbergen, N. 1953. *Social Behavior in Animals*. New York: Wiley.

Tobias, Sheila. 1978. *Overcoming Math Anxiety*. New York: Norton.

Tonkinson, Robert. 1978. *The Mardudjara Aborigines: Living the Dream in Australia's Desert*. New York: Holt, Rinehart and Winston.

Turnbull, Colin M. 1961. The Forest People. New York: Simon and Schuster.

Ullock, B., and N. Wagner. 1980. "The Evolution of Human Sexual Behavior." In *The Evolution of Human Social Behavior*, edited by J. Lockard. New York: Elsevier.

Van Den Berghe, P. 1979. *Human Family Systems: An Evolutionary View*. New York: Elsevier.

———. 1980. "The Human Family: A Sociobiological Look." In *The Evolution of Human Social Behavior*, edited by J. Lockard. New York: Elsevier.

Waddington, C. H. 1957. *The Strategy of the Genes: A Discussion of Aspects of Theoretical Biology*. London: Allen and Unwin.

Washburn, S., and I. DeVore. 1961. "The Social Life of Baboons." *Scientific American* 204 (6): 61–71.

Washburn, S., and D. Hamburg. 1965. "The Study of Primate Behavior." In *Primate Behavior*, edited by I. DeVore. New York: Holt, Rinehart and Winston.

Wilson, E. O. 1975. *Sociobology: The New Synthesis*. Cambridge: Harvard University Press.

Witkin, H. A. 1973. *The Role of Cognitive Style in Academic Performance and in Teacher-Student Relations*. Princeton, N.J.: Educational Testing Service.

Wobst, H. M. 1978. "The Archaeo-Ethnology of Hunter-Gatherers; or, the Tyranny of the Ethnographic Record in Archaeology." *American Antiquity* 43 (2): 303–9.

Index